Nine Words that Change Everything

ROSS C POWELL

Copyright Notice

Copyright © 2025, ROSS C POWELL.

All rights reserved. No part of this publication may be copied, reproduced, republished, translated, stored, or transmitted in any form or by any means—whether electronic, mechanical, digital, or otherwise - without the prior written permission of the publisher.

This book is the result of dedication, creativity, and countless hours of effort. Any resemblance to real persons, living or dead, is purely coincidental—or perhaps just the universe having a bit of fun.

Published by Kinetic Digital Publishers

www.kineticdigitalpublishers.com

For permissions, inquiries, or other correspondence, please visit our website.

TABLE OF CONTENTS

Preface 1

Introduction 3
   The Power of Nine Words in a Noisy World 3

Chapter 1 6
   The Foundation: Propitiation The Atoning Sacrifice of Christ.... 6

Chapter 2: 14
   Praise – The Heartbeat of Christian Worship 14

Chapter 3: 20
   Provision – God's Faithfulness in Every Season 20

Chapter 4: 27
   Protection – Divine Safeguarding in Perilous Times 27

Chapter 5: 35
   Peace – Christ's Unshakable Gift in a Troubled World 35

Chapter 6: 45
   Promise – The Certainty of God's Word in an Uncertain World 45

Chapter 7: 54
   Power – The Demonstration of God's Strength in Human Weakness 54

Chapter 8: 62
   Perseverance – Remaining Steadfast in Faith Despite Hardships 62

Chapter 9: 76
   Presence – Experiencing the Nearness of God in Everyday Life .. 76

Chapter 10:..**88**
   Living the Nine Words 88
Conclusion..**91**
Afterword..**95**

Preface

Let me ask you something: ***What words define your walk with God?***

I've found that in the noise of modern life, with its endless distractions, half-truths, and fleeting comforts—many of us struggle to articulate what it really means to follow Jesus. We know bits and pieces, but we lack a clear, cohesive understanding of how grace works itself out in our daily lives.

That's why I've written this book around **nine words**—nine foundational truths that, when taken together, give us a full-orbed picture of the Christian life. These aren't just theological terms; they're the living, breathing realities that sustain real faith in the real world.

Why These Nine Words?

Imagine building a house without a blueprint. You might get walls up, but will they hold when the storm hits? In the same way, many believers today have a fragmented faith—a collection of inspiring ideas but no sturdy framework to make sense of suffering, doubt, or even joy.

These nine words are that framework.

They start with **propitiation**, because without the cross, nothing else makes sense. From there, they move to **praise**, because once you grasp what Christ has done, worship isn't optional—it's inevitable. Then comes **provision**, because our Father doesn't save us and then leave us to fend for ourselves. **Protection** reminds us that no matter what happens, our souls are eternally secure. **Peace** steadies us when life feels chaotic. **Promise** anchors us to hope when everything seems uncertain. **Power** fuels us when we're running on empty. **Perseverance** proves our faith is real, not just a passing emotion. And

presence—ah, presence—assures us we're never alone, because God isn't a distant idea; He's with us, here and now. **What You'll Find in These Pages**

This isn't a book of abstract theory. Each chapter takes one of these words and unpacks it in a way that's both deeply biblical and intensely practical. You'll discover:

- *How these truths fit together*—like interlocking pieces that form a complete picture of God's work in your life.

- *Where we often go wrong*—the subtle counterfeits that sneak in and dilute real faith.

- *Practical ways to live this out*—because truth isn't just for studying; it's for living.

Who This Book Is

Whether you're a new believer trying to make sense of your faith or a seasoned saint looking for fresh encouragement, these nine words are for you. They're for the weary parent praying through sleepless nights, the student navigating doubts, the worker striving to honor Christ in a secular workplace—for anyone who wants more than a shallow spirituality.

A Personal Invitation

As you read, I hope you'll do more than underline sentences. I hope you'll pause, reflect, and let these truths sink deep. Because when these nine words move from your head to your heart, something beautiful happens: your faith stops feeling like a burden and starts feeling like what it really is, a lifeline, a hope, a home. Being fully known and fully loved.

So let's begin. There's a journey ahead, and it's one worth taking.

Introduction

The Power of Nine Words in a Noisy World

We live in an age drowning in words. Never before in human history have we been so saturated with information, yet so starved for wisdom. Social media feeds scroll endlessly, news cycles spin 24/7, and digital chatter floods our minds from the moment we wake until we collapse into bed exhausted. In this relentless barrage of content, opinions, and hot takes, one profound truth gets lost: **Jesus spoke with revolutionary simplicity.**

What if, in this era of overwhelming noise, we pressed pause on the chaos to focus on just **nine words**—short, powerful, life-shaping truths that cut through the confusion of modern life? These aren't random words or trendy slogans. They are **foundational, time-tested truths** that have anchored believers for centuries yet remain startlingly relevant today.

This book is not about reducing Christianity to soundbites. Rather, it's about **rediscovering the concentrated power of biblical truth**—truth so potent that a single word from God can:

- **Silence a storm** (Mark 4:39)
- **Heal a broken body** (Matthew 8:8)
- **Raise the dead** (John 11:43)
- **Forgive sins** (Luke 7:48)
- **Transform eternity** (Luke 23:43)

Each of these nine words serves as:

1. **An Anchor** - Stabilizing your soul when cultural currents try to sweep you away
2. **A Filter** - Helping you discern truth in an age of endless opinions
3. **A Compass** - Guiding your decisions when the path isn't clear
4. **A Weapon** - Equipping you for the spiritual battles you face daily
5. **A Mirror** - Revealing areas where your life needs to align with God's Word

Some of these words will **comfort you** in your struggles. Others will **confront areas** where you've compromised. All of them will **reorient your perspective** to see yourself, your relationships, and your world through God's eyes.

Why This Matters Now More Than Ever

We're living in what one historian called "the age of attention fragmentation." Our minds are pulled in countless directions while our souls grow malnourished on spiritual fast food. Many Christians today can:

- Quote dozens of movie lines but struggle to recall Scripture
- Navigate complex apps yet feel lost in basic prayer
- Debate politics passionately but falter in explaining the gospel simply

This book is a corrective to that imbalance. It's not about dumbing down faith, but about **concentrating on what's essential**. Just as a magnifying glass focuses sunlight into burning intensity, these nine words focus divine truth into transformative power for your:

- **Thought life** (renewing your mind)
- **Emotional health** (guarding your heart)
- **Relationships** (loving others well)
- **Vocation** (working with purpose)
- **Stewardship** (managing resources wisely)
- **Witness** (sharing Christ effectively)

How to Use This Book

1. **Read reflectively** - These aren't truths to skim but to savor
2. **Apply practically** - Each chapter ends with actionable steps
3. **Share communally** - Discuss these words with your small group
4. **Return frequently** - Let this be a reference you revisit

Whether you're:

- A new believer seeking solid footing
- A longtime Christian needing refreshment
- A ministry leader looking for simple yet profound teaching tools
- Someone spiritually searching for what's real…these nine words offer **clarity in confusion, peace in chaos, and direction in disorientation.**

Jesus promised, "The truth will set you free" (John 8:32). In a world of chains—anxiety, addiction, aimlessness, anger—**freedom comes not from more information, but from the right revelation.** These nine words are your gateway to that liberation.

Let's begin the journey.

Chapter 1

The Foundation: Propitiation The Atoning Sacrifice of Christ

I. What Propitiation Really Means (And Why It Changes Everything)

Let's talk about a word that might sound intimidating but is actually the most beautiful truth in the Bible - propitiation. At its core, it's God's brilliant solution to the biggest problem in the universe: how can a perfectly holy God forgive sinful people like us without compromising His justice?

The Greek word behind it (**hilasmos**) paints this vivid picture: imagine righteous anger being satisfied, wrath being turned away, through a substitute taking the punishment. This isn't like human anger that flares up unpredictably. God's wrath is different - it's His settled, righteous opposition to sin because He's perfectly just (Romans 1:18). And here's the sobering truth: we all deserve that wrath (John 3:36). Left to ourselves, there's no way back to God.

Now here's where it gets fascinating. God gave us a preview of this solution way back in the Old Testament. On the Day of Atonement (Leviticus 16), the high priest would sacrifice a flawless goat and sprinkle its blood on the Ark's mercy seat. This was God's temporary system - the blood covering Israel's sins and turning away wrath for another year. But here's the catch: animal blood could never fully deal with sin (Hebrews 10:4). It was like a placeholder, pointing ahead to something greater.

Then Jesus steps onto the scene, and John the Baptist, this wild, locust-eating prophet, takes one look at Him and declares with prophetic certainty: "Behold, the Lamb of God who takes away the sin of the world!" (John 1:29). In that moment, centuries of sacrificial rituals suddenly snap into focus. Every lamb slain on Passover, every drop of blood spilled at the altar, every trembling sinner laying hands on a scapegoat—they were all pointing to Him.

But here's what blows my mind: Jesus didn't just fulfill the sacrificial system, He redefined it. The book of Hebrews unpacks this in stunning detail:

- **No more temporary fixes** → Animal sacrifices had to be repeated "year after year" (Hebrews 10:1-4), but Jesus offered "one sacrifice for sins forever" (Hebrews 10:12).

- **No more symbolic covering** → The blood of bulls and goats could only cover sin (the Hebrew word kaphar means "atonement"), but Christ's blood removes it (John 1:29 uses the Greek word airō—to take away completely).

- **No more separation** → Under the old system, only the high priest could enter the Holy of Holies—and only once a year. But when Jesus died, the temple veil tore from top to bottom (Mark 15:38), signaling open access to God for all who come through Christ.

This wasn't just a nice moral example or a tragic martyr's death. This was cosmic justice at work. Isaiah 53:5-6,10 paints the brutal reality:

"He was pierced for our transgressions, crushed for our iniquities... the Lord laid on Him the iniquity of us all... It was the Lord's will to crush Him."

Let that sink in. On the cross:

- **The Judge became the Substitute**
- **The Innocent bore the guilty's penalty**
- **The Wrath-Magnifier became the Wrath-Absorber**

That's propitiation—the satisfaction of God's holy wrath against sin through the perfect sacrifice of His Son (Romans 3:25; 1 John 2:2). It's the ultimate divine exchange:

"For our sake He made Him to be sin who knew no sin, so that in Him we might become the righteousness of God" (2 Corinthians 5:21).

And here's why this changes everything for you today:

1. **Your guilt has an expiration date** → In Christ, God isn't keeping score (Psalm 103:12).

2. **Your failures aren't final** → The same power that conquered sin on the cross is now at work in you (Romans 8:11).

3. **Your future is secure** → If God didn't spare His own Son, how will He not also "graciously give us all things"? (Romans 8:32).

This is the foundation everything else builds on. No propitiation? No peace. No pardon. No power. But because of the cross, we can walk in radical freedom: not as those trying to earn God's favor, but as those already lavishly loved and renewed.

II. Breaking Down Propitiation: Why It Matters

A. Why We Needed Propitiation

Let's get real for a minute - God's perfect holiness can't just wink at sin (Habakkuk 1:13). That would be like a judge letting a murderer go free because he's a nice guy. Justice demands payment. The Old Testament shows this repeatedly - sin equals death (Ezekiel 18:4), and forgiveness requires blood (Leviticus 17:11). Those animal sacrifices? They were like IOUs - temporary fixes pointing forward to the real solution (Hebrews 10:4).

Then Jesus shows up. Here's what makes His sacrifice different: He's both perfect God and perfect man. Only He could bear the infinite weight of God's wrath that we deserved (2 Corinthians 5:21). When He cried "My God, why have you forsaken me?" (Matthew 27:46), that was Him experiencing the hell we should have faced. This wasn't just physical torture - this was God's righteous anger against sin being poured out on Jesus instead of us (Romans 3:25-26).

B. God's Amazing Plan

Here's what blows my mind - this wasn't our idea. In pagan religions, people try to appease angry gods with sacrifices and rituals. But our God? He made the first move. The Father sent the Son to be our propitiation (1 John 4:10). While we were still shaking our fists at God, He was planning our rescue (Romans 5:8).

This is the Trinity in action:

- **The Father demands justice and provides the sacrifice**
- **The Son willingly offers Himself (Hebrews 9:14)**
- **The Spirit applies this salvation to us (Romans 8:3-4)**

The result? God stays perfectly just while making us right with Him. As Paul puts it, He's both "just and the justifier" (Romans 3:26). Mind = blown.

C. Fake Versions to Watch Out For on a Daily Basis

Lots of people try to water this down today. Here's what to watch for:

1. **The "Good Example" Theory** - Says Jesus' death was just to show us how much God loves us. Problem? It ignores that God's wrath needed to be satisfied (Galatians 3:13). Without that, the cross loses its power.

2. **The "Divine Object Lesson" Theory** - Claims Jesus died to show how serious sin is, not actually to pay for it. Makes the cross more like a protest sign than an actual solution.

3. **The "Everyone's Automatically Saved" Error** - Says Christ's death saves all people whether they believe or not (John 3:36). Turns the gospel into a meaningless blanket statement.

4. **The "DIY Salvation" Scam** - Thinks our good deeds or suffering can make up for our sin. But Acts 4:12 is clear - there's only one name that saves.

Real propitiation? It's Jesus taking our punishment - actually, specifically, completely. That's the gospel that changes everything.

III. How Propitiation Changes Everything in Your Daily Life

Let's get practical. This isn't just theology for the classroom—it's truth that should rock your world every single day.

1. You Can Stop Doubting Your Salvation

Here's the deal: If Christ's death fully satisfied God's wrath for your sin (and it did), then your standing with God isn't based on how good you're doing this week. It's based on Jesus' finished work (Hebrews 10:14). That means when guilt creeps in or Satan whispers, "You're not good enough," you can point straight to the cross and say, "But Jesus was—and He's mine." (Romans 8:1)

2. Worship Will Hit Different

Once it really sinks in that Jesus took the hell you deserved, singing "Amazing Grace" stops being just nice lyrics—it becomes a heart explosion. The Lord's Supper? That's not just a ritual; it's a tangible reminder that the wrath you should've faced was swallowed up in love (1 Corinthians 11:26). Prayer becomes less about begging and more about running to the Father who already went to insane lengths to bring you home (1 John 4:19).

3. You'll Actually Want to Share the Gospel

Most of us tip-toe around evangelism because we're afraid of offending people. But if you really believe your unsaved neighbor is headed for eternal separation from God (John 3:18), how could you stay silent? Propitiation gives us urgency—not to scare people, but to plead with them, "There's a way out! Jesus already paid for you!"

4. Sin Starts to Lose Its Grip

Here's a gut-check: Every time we choose sin, we're basically saying, "This is worth more than what Jesus did for me." But when you marinate in the truth that Christ suffered unimaginably to free you from sin's penalty, power, and (one day) presence—it makes that temporary pleasure way less appealing (Romans 6:1-2). Holiness isn't about rule-following; it's the only reasonable response to being bought at such a crazy high price (1 Peter 1:18-19).

IV. Why This Truth is Non-Negotiable in Our Lives

In a world obsessed with self-help spirituality, we've got to hold tight to this: The cross wasn't a suggestion—it was the only solution to the wrath problem. Don't soften the blow ("You're basically good!") or skip to the feel-good parts. The bad news (we're sinners deserving wrath) makes the good news (Jesus took it for us) explode with meaning.

Your Move:

- **Memorize 1 John 2:2 and Romans 3:25-26**—armor against doubt.
- **Study Leviticus 16 and Isaiah 53**. Those ancient sacrifices? They're like God's 4K trailer for Jesus' coming.
- **Tell Someone this week**—not just that "Jesus loves you," but that He saved you from God's wrath. That's the game-changer.
- **Worship Harder than ever**. You're singing as someone who should be condemned but is forever loved instead.

The cross is where the unthinkable happened: Justice got exactly what it demanded, and mercy got exactly what it desired. That's not just good theology—that's your lifeboat, your anthem, and your hope until the day you see Him face to face. Now go live like you believe it.

Chapter 2:

Praise – The Heartbeat of Christian Worship

I. What Praise Really Is (And Why It's a Big Deal)

Let's talk about praise—not just the "say-God-is-good-before-dinner" kind, but the full-throttle, can't-help-but-shout-it kind of praise that the Bible shows us. At its core, praise is our explosive response to who God is and what He's done. It's not some optional add-on to faith; it's the instinctive reaction of anyone who's truly encountered Him.

The Bible's Vocabulary of Praise

The Old Testament gives us a bunch of words for praise, each with its own flavor:

- **Halal** (הלל) (where we get "hallelujah") means to go wild with joy about God—like when your team wins the championship and you're screaming your head off. Psalm 113:1 is basically saying, "Y'all—stop everything and celebrate the Lord!"

- **Yadah** (יָדָה) is praise with your whole body—hands lifted, voice loud, heart wide open. Picture Psalm 100:4: "Walk into God's presence like you mean it, with thanks on your lips and praise in your posture."

- **Zamar** (זָמַר) is musical worship—belting out songs, clapping, maybe even dancing (Psalm 98:4-5). It's not about perfect pitch; it's about unfiltered joy.

Then in the New Testament, proskyneō describes worship so awe-filled you'd bow to the ground. Jesus told the Samaritan woman this is the kind of worship God wants—raw, real, and rooted in truth (John 4:23).

Praise Isn't Just a Human Thing

Here's the crazy part: We're not the only ones praising God. The stars are doing it (Psalm 19:1). Angels never stop (Isaiah 6:3). Even Jesus—hours from the cross—was singing hymns with His disciples (Matthew 26:30). The early church? They turned everyday life into a praise party (Acts 2:47).

So praise isn't just something we do. It's what we're made for. When we get who God really is, praise isn't forced—it just spills out.

II. Why Praise is Way More Powerful Than You Think

Let's be real—praise isn't just singing nice songs in church. It's a weapon, a game-changer, and a full-on rebellion against the darkness of our world.

A. Praise is Spiritual Warfare (And It Actually Works)

Ever heard the story in 2 Chronicles 20? King Jehoshaphat's army was totally outmatched, but God told him to do something wild: Send the worship team out first. No swords, no strategy—just singers belting, "His love endures forever!" And guess what? The enemy armies freaked out and started killing each other.

Here's the takeaway: Praise isn't just noise—it's warfare.

Fast-forward to today. Our battles might look different (think ideological chaos, digital lies, and straight-up demonic garbage), but the weapon's the same. Psalm 8:2 says even baby's praise shuts down the enemy. When Paul and Silas sang in jail, their chains shattered (Acts 16:25-26). That's not a metaphor—praise literally shakes the spiritual realm.

B. Praise is God's Favorite Place to Show Up

Psalm 22:3 says God is "enthroned on the praises" of His people. That means when we praise, He moves in. It's like flipping a switch—He promises when we draw near, He does too (James 4:8).

But let's be clear: This isn't about chasing emotional highs.

Modern worship can sometimes feel like a concert—lights, vibes, and a killer vocal run. But real praise isn't about us feeling something. It's about Him being everything. Revelation 5:12 nails it: Jesus is worthy—full stop. Not because of what He does for us, but because of who He is.

C. Don't Fall for Fake Praise

Our culture's packed with cheap imitations:

- **Entertainment worship:** Services that feel more like a show than surrender.
- **Performative spirituality:** Posting "praise hands" on social media while your heart's MIA.
- **Self-help gratitude:** Journals that turn thankfulness into a therapy hack instead of God-focused awe.

Real praise? It's unshakable. It doesn't need perfect circumstances—just a heart that knows God is good, even when life isn't. It's not about us getting pumped up; it's about Him being lifted high.

So next time you praise, remember: You're not just singing—you're fighting, inviting God's presence, and rejecting every counterfeit this world tries to sell you.

III. How to Make Praise a Real-Life Thing (Not Just a Sunday Thing)

Let's get practical—how do we actually live this out in our crazy, distracted world?

A. Making Praise Your Daily Habit

The psalmist wasn't kidding when he said, "I'll praise God nonstop" (Psalm 34:1). But how?

1. **Start your day with praise, not panic.** Before you grab your phone or doomscroll the news, hit pause. Try Psalm 92's method: "God, Your love is my first thought today. Your faithfulness is my last thought tonight." It's like spiritual caffeine—it wakes your soul up right.

2. **Praise when it hurts.** Job's kids died, his wealth vanished, and his first response was worship (Job 1:21). That's next-level. When anxiety creeps in, try singing truth instead of spiraling. Even if it's through gritted teeth—"God's still good" changes the atmosphere (Colossians 3:16).

3. **Show up with your people.** Online church is convenient, but Hebrews 10:25 says physical presence matters. There's power in real voices harmonizing, real shoulders to cry on, real high-fives when God moves. Don't Netflix-church your way through life.

B. Praise in a Tech-Distracted World

Our phones are double-edged swords for worship:

- **Good: You've got worship playlists for your commute, sermons on demand, and the Bible in your pocket.**
- **Danger: It's easy to consume faith content without ever engaging with God.**

Jesus called out the "lip-service crew" (Matthew 15:8)—people who post #Blessed but live stressed. If your Instagram worship doesn't match your private life, it's just performance. Use tech as a tool, not a substitute for real connection with God.

C. Raising Kids Who Actually Love Worship

Parents, listen up: Kids won't catch authentic praise by accident. Deuteronomy 6:7 says to weave faith into everyday life. Here's how:

- Explain the "why" behind songs. Don't just sing "10,000 Reasons"—talk about the 10,000 things God's done for your family. Make worship a conversation, not a chore.
- Tell stories of radical praise. Share how persecuted believers sang in prison cells or how missionaries praised God in impossible situations. Make it heroic.
- Swap screen zombies for worship warriors. Limit mind-numbing YouTube. Fill your home with Scripture songs instead. Dance in the kitchen. Pray out loud. Let them see you mean it when you worship.

Bottom line: Praise isn't a mood—it's a muscle. The more you use it, the stronger your faith gets. Start small, but start today.

IV. Why Praise Never Ends (And Why That Matters for Everyday)

Here's the wild truth: The praise we start here? It's just the warm-up. Heaven's going to be one never-ending, full-volume worship session (Revelation 7:9-12). Picture this—every nation, tribe, and language shouting together: "Salvation belongs to our God!" What we practice now is basically eternity prep.

This year, we've got a choice to make:

Will we be like the Israelites—grumbling about every problem, stuck in complaint mode? Or like David, who decided before anything happened: "I'm praising God no matter what" (Psalm 34:1)?

Today's world might get darker, but that just means the Church's light should burn brighter. And guess what fuels that fire? Praise.

Your Move:

1. **Lock Psalm 145 in your heart.** Make it your personal anthem.
2. **Swap screens for worship.** Try a week without Netflix—replace it with raw, real worship and Scripture. (Trust me, you'll survive.)
3. **Tell someone what God's done.** Your story of His faithfulness might be the hope someone desperately needs.

Here's the bottom line: Praise isn't just something we do—it's who we are when Jesus is really our everything. So let's live like we mean it. The echo of our praise today will keep ringing long after the year, decade, or century is over. Let's make it count.

Chapter 3:

Provision – God's Faithfulness in Every Season

I. What Does "God Will Provide" Really Mean?

Let's talk about how God takes care of His people—because it's way bigger than just paying bills or putting food on the table. The Bible shows us God's provision is everything—physical needs, emotional strength, spiritual nourishment, the whole package.

Remember that famous name Jehovah Jireh ("The Lord Will Provide")? It first shows up when Abraham's about to sacrifice Isaac, and God steps in at the last second with a ram (Genesis 22:14). That moment wasn't just about solving Abraham's immediate problem—it revealed something permanent about God's character: He sees what we need before we do, and He's already got it covered.

Now check out how God provides:

- **The wild, miraculous stuff:** Bread falling from the sky (Exodus 16), birds delivering takeout to Elijah (1 Kings 17:6)—God loves showing off His power when ordinary solutions won't cut it.

- **The everyday, built-into-creation stuff:** Rain for crops (Leviticus 26:4), skills to do your job well (Proverbs 8:12-21), people who've got your back (Acts 2:44-45). Most of the time, God works through normal means—but that doesn't make it any less His provision.

Jesus put it perfectly when He said, "Don't waste your life worrying about food or clothes. Your Father already knows what you need" (Matthew 6:31-32). That word "provide" in Greek isn't about scrambling last-minute—it means God's ahead of the need, planning exactly how to meet it.

So whether it's a miracle or a paycheck, a sudden breakthrough or slow-and-steady grace—it's all Him. And that changes how we live.

II. Digging Deeper: What the Bible Really Says About God's Provision

A. God's Provision = His Promise in Action

God's care for us isn't random—it's part of His unbreakable covenant. When He fed Israel with manna in the desert (Deuteronomy 8:3), it wasn't just about filling bellies. It was a daily object lesson: "Life depends on My word, not your efforts." Fast forward to Jesus, who called Himself the real Bread from heaven (John 6:32)—showing that God's ultimate provision is Himself.

Here's the 2025 takeaway: Stock markets crash. Supply chains fail. But God's faithfulness? Never fluctuates. Psalm 37:25 isn't a prosperity promise ("You'll get rich!"), but a rock-solid assurance: "If you put My kingdom first, you won't starve." (Matthew 6:33).

B. Why God Lets Us Run Empty

Some of the Bible's biggest provision miracles start with nothing left:
- A widow with literally her last meal (1 Kings 17:7-16)
- A kid's lunchbox with five loaves and two fish (John 6:1-14)

God keeps letting His people hit rock bottom to expose our modern idols:

- **Hoarding ("I need a 6-month pantry")**
- **Self-sufficiency ("I've got this under control")**
- **Entitlement ("I deserve comfort")**

His method? Daily bread (Exodus 16:4)—not a 401(k). In our Amazon Prime, instant-gratification world, learning to depend on Him each morning is radical discipleship.

C. Dodging the "Name It and Claim It" Trap

Beware of preachers who turn God into a vending machine: "Just believe hard enough, and you'll get rich!" That's not Christianity—it's spiritualized greed. Jesus warned His followers would suffer (Luke 9:23), and Paul knew both hunger and full stomachs (Philippians 4:12).

Real provision looks like:

- Being okay when the bank account's low (Hebrews 13:5)
- Finding strength in weakness (2 Corinthians 12:9)
- Using blessings to bless others (1 Timothy 6:17-19)

God's not a sugar daddy. He's a Father who gives exactly what we need—whether that's a miracle or the grace to endure the trial.

III. Practical Ways to Trust God's Provision in Uncertain Times

Let's be real—life feels unstable right now. Prices keep climbing, jobs feel shaky, and the news cycle constantly warns of the next crisis. But here's the truth that changes everything: **God is still our provider.** He hasn't forgotten us, and His promises haven't expired.

So, how do we live this out in 2024? Here are seven practical ways to anchor our lives in God's faithfulness—not fear.

1. Make Tithing Your First Act of Worship

Tithing isn't just a religious duty—it's a declaration. When we give God the first 10% of our income (Malachi 3:10), we're saying, *"You own it all, and I trust You with it."*

But here's the challenge: In a world of autopay and digital transactions, giving can become impersonal. So let's make it intentional. Before you pay bills or budget for groceries, pause. Set aside that first portion with a prayer: *"God, this is Yours. Use it for Your kingdom."*

Why does this matter? Because tithing trains our hearts to depend on **God, not our paycheck.** It reminds us that every dollar we have is a gift from Him—and He's never failed to provide for His children.

2. Pray Specifically—Then Watch God Work

Jesus taught us to pray, *"Give us this day our daily bread"* (Matthew 6:11). That's a radical prayer in a culture obsessed with stockpiling and self-sufficiency.

Here's a practical way to live this out: **Keep a "Provision Journal."** Write down your needs—big and small—and leave space to record how God answers. Maybe it's an unexpected check in the mail, a discount at the grocery store, or a friend who shows up at just the right time.

When financial anxiety hits (and it will), flip through that journal. Remind yourself: *"God came through before—He'll do it again."* This isn't about positive thinking; it's about **remembering His faithfulness** (Philippians 4:6).

3. Be Radically Generous—Even When It Feels Risky

The early church turned heads because they shared everything (Acts 4:32-35). That kind of generosity is still counter cultural today. So, how do we live this out?

- **Keep a "blessing stash"**—extra nonperishables, toiletries, or cash set aside specifically to give.
- **Look for the overlooked**—single parents, widows, struggling families—and ask, *"How can I help?"*—time, skills, a listening ear.

Generosity isn't just about writing checks; it's about **living open-handed.** When we share what we have, we prove that God's economy operates differently from the world's.

4. Know the Difference Between Needs and Wants

Our culture blurs the line between "I need this" and "I want this." But Paul's words cut through the noise: "If we have food and clothing, with these we will be content" (1 Timothy 6:8).

1. **Try this: Conduct a monthly "heart check" on your spending. Ask: Is this a true need or just a desire?**
2. **Does this reflect God's priorities or the world's?**

Then simplify where you can. Teach your kids by involving them in decisions—like choosing to give to a family in need instead of buying another toy. Contentment isn't about deprivation; it's about finding joy in what truly matters.

5. Develop Skills—But Don't Worship Your Career

Work is good—God often provides through our jobs (Proverbs 22:29). But in an unstable economy, we can't treat careers like our security. So **learn practical skills**—budgeting, basic repairs, gardening—not because God might fail you, but because He's given you a mind to steward well. And if layoffs come? Remember Elijah (1 Kings 17:3-6). When royal provisions dried up, God fed him through ravens. Your career isn't your source—**God is.**

6. Be Prudent, Not Paranoid

There's a difference between wisdom and fear. Scripture warns against hoarding (Luke 12:15-21) but commends preparation (Proverbs 6:6-8). So keep reasonable supplies—but regularly give away the excess. If shortages happen, let your response point people to God. Panic says, *"I'm on my own."* Faith says, *"My Father owns the cattle on a thousand hills"* (Psalm 50:10).

7. Teach the Next Generation Where Real Security Lies

Kids growing up in a "buy now, pay later" culture need to know: **True security isn't in stuff—it's in God.**

- **Involve them in giving**—let them pick toys to donate or help pack blessing bags.
- **Share stories of God's faithfulness**—like George Müller, who fed orphans through prayer alone.
- **Watch your language**—swap *"We can't afford it"* with *"Let's ask God if this is His best for us."*

Model contentment by valuing **people over possessions.** Show them that life with God is an adventure—not a spreadsheet.

Final Challenge:

God's provision isn't a theory—it's a daily reality. The crazier the world gets, the more our lives should shout: *"My God supplies all I need!"* (Philippians 4:19). So this week, pick **one practical step** from this list and act on it. Then watch what God does.

Who's ready to live like we actually trust Him? Let's go!

IV. Conclusion: The Bread of Life and Our Daily Trust

Jesus' declaration, "I am the bread of life" (John 6:35), redefines provision. Our greatest need is not material but relational—union with Christ, the true sustainer. As any year or day can have its economic challenges, may we embody the psalmist's confidence: "The Lord is my shepherd; I shall not want" (Psalm 23:1).

Action Steps for the Year Ahead:

1. **Conduct a spending audit**—Identify one area (e.g., groceries, entertainment) and reallocate 10% to purposeful giving.

2. **Memorize Philippians 4:19**—"And my God will supply every need of yours according to His riches in glory in Christ Jesus." Recite it when anxiety arises.

3. **Fast from complaining about lack**—For one week, replace every grumble with thanksgiving for past provision.

God's faithfulness has never been measured by bank balances but by His covenant promises. In lack or abundance, His grace is sufficient—will we trust Him?

Chapter 4:

Protection – Divine Safeguarding in Perilous Times

I. What Does the Bible Really Mean by "Protection"?

Let's talk about what it means that God protects us—because it might not be what you think.

You know that feeling when you're walking through a rough neighborhood at night, and suddenly you see a police car roll by? That little surge of relief? That's a tiny picture of what the Bible shows us about God's protection. The Hebrew word shamar (שָׁמַר) pops up over 400 times in the Old Testament—it means God is actively keeping watch over us, like a shepherd guarding sheep or a soldier standing post.

When God told Abraham, "I am your shield" (Genesis 15:1), He wasn't making a casual promise. He was establishing something fundamental about how He relates to His people. And here's the crazy part—this protection wasn't because Abraham had it all together. It was because God is faithful.

We see this play out all through Scripture:

- **Physical protection:** Daniel spending the night with hungry lions and walking out without a scratch (Daniel 6:22)
- **Spiritual armor:** Paul's description of God's full-body armor to stand against spiritual attacks (Ephesians 6:10-18)

- **Emotional safety:** That supernatural peace that guards your heart when everything's falling apart (Philippians 4:7)

But—and this is important—God's protection doesn't mean we get a free pass from hard things. Paul got beaten, shipwrecked, and thrown in prison (2 Corinthians 11:23-28). Jesus straight-up told His guys, "In this world, you're gonna have trouble" (John 16:33).

So here's the bottom line: Biblical protection isn't about avoiding the storm—it's about who's in the boat with you. It's not a force field against pain; it's the unshakable promise that no matter what hits, God's holding you, strengthening you, and working it for your good.

That's the kind of protection worth building your life on.

II. Digging Deeper: What Does Real Protection Look Like?

Let's get honest—when we hear "God protects us," we often picture a force field that keeps bad things from touching us. But the Bible paints a much richer, sometimes surprising picture of what divine protection really means.

A. God's Protection is a Promise—Not a Magic Trick

The Psalms are packed with wild promises about God's protection. We read that *"God's angels set up camp around His people"* (Psalm 34:7) and that *"no plague even comes near your house"* (Psalm 91:10). But here's the catch—these aren't blank checks to claim immunity from life's struggles. They're invitations to trust the *Person* behind the promises.

Think about Jesus in the wilderness when Satan dared Him to jump off the temple, quoting Scripture about angels catching Him. Jesus refused, saying, *"You shall not put the Lord your God to the test"*

(Matthew 4:7). Why? Because real faith doesn't *test* God; it *trusts* Him—whether He intervenes dramatically or sustains us quietly.

For us today, this means when fear creeps in, we can pray Psalm 91 *not* like a magic spell, but as a reminder: *"God, You're my safe place."* Protection isn't about controlling outcomes; it's about clinging to the One who controls everything.

B. The Mystery: Protection In the Fire, Not Always From It

One of the most profound truths about God's protection is that it often operates *within* suffering rather than eliminating it. Take Shadrach, Meshach, and Abednego—they didn't get a last-minute pardon from the fiery furnace. They walked *into* the flames and met Jesus *there* (Daniel 3:25). Their deliverance came *through* the trial, not apart from it.

We see this pattern all through Scripture. Paul begged God three times to remove his *"thorn in the flesh"*—some chronic pain or weakness. But God answered, *"My grace is sufficient for you, for My power is made perfect in weakness"* (2 Corinthians 12:9). Even Jesus told His disciples, *"Not a hair on your head will perish"* (Luke 21:18)— right before warning them they'd face persecution and even death!

What does this mean for us today, especially as believers face increasing hostility toward biblical values? It means our safety isn't in avoiding pain but in knowing *nothing*—not job loss, illness, or persecution—can snatch us from God's hand (John 10:28). If God allows hardship, it's not because He failed. It's because He's doing something *deeper* than comfort—He's shaping us into Christ's image.

C. Spotting Fake "Protection" in a Spiritual Supermarket

Our world is full of counterfeits when it comes to divine protection. First, there's the ***prosperity gospel trap***—the idea that if you just have enough faith, you'll never suffer. But Jesus didn't promise His followers a life of ease; He said, *"Take up your cross and follow Me"* (Matthew 16:24). Real faith prepares us for both abundance *and* hardship.

Then there's **fatalism**—the mindset that says, *"Why lock my doors? God will protect me!"* But that's not faith; it's foolishness. Even Jesus avoided unnecessary risks, slipping away when crowds tried to throw Him off a cliff (Luke 4:29-30). God expects us to use wisdom while trusting His sovereignty.

And let's not forget the **occult hacks**—rituals, chants, or attempts to *"bind"* evil spirits through formulas rather than relying on Christ's finished work. The Bible is clear: *"He disarmed the rulers and authorities and put them to open shame, by triumphing over them in Him"* (Colossians 2:15). We don't need gimmicks; we have Jesus.

So, what does true biblical protection look like? It's about staying *connected* to Christ like a branch to a vine (John 15:4), filling our minds with Scripture so truth becomes our armor (Psalm 119:114), and making wise choices while resting in God's ultimate control (Proverbs 2:7-8).

Bottom Line: God's protection isn't about avoiding storms—it's about who's *in the boat* with you. When the waves hit, He might calm them... or He might let them rage while proving He's enough to keep you from drowning. Either way, *you're safe.* That's the kind of security worth building your life on.

III. Living Out God's Protection in Everyday Life

Let's be real—we're living in crazy times. Between the chaos in the news, the pressure of social media, and the uncertainty of the future, it's easy to feel overwhelmed. But here's the good news: God's protection isn't just a nice idea—it's a reality we can live in every single day. So, how do we actually do that? Let's break it down.

1. Building a Life of Unshakable Trust

It all starts with where we place our confidence. Every morning, before we even check our phones or dive into the day's worries, we need to anchor our hearts in truth. Psalm 27:1 says, *"The Lord is my light and my salvation—whom shall I fear?"* That's not just a nice verse—it's a battle cry. When anxiety tries to creep in, we don't just sit there and take it. We speak God's promises out loud: *"You are my hiding place; You will protect me from trouble"* (Psalm 32:7). This isn't positive thinking—it's declaring reality over our fears. Because God's protection doesn't depend on our circumstances; it depends on *who He is.*

2. Fighting Spiritual Battles in a Digital World

Let's not kid ourselves—the real battles we face aren't just against people or politics. Ephesians 6:12 makes it clear: *"Our struggle is not against flesh and blood, but against the rulers, against the authorities, against the powers of this dark world."* And in our modern life, those battles are playing out online, in the media, and in the cultural narratives trying to redefine truth.

So, how do we stand firm? By putting on *all* of God's armor—not just the pieces we like. Truth has to be our foundation in a world full of lies. Righteousness—living with integrity—has to be our compass when compromise is everywhere. The gospel of peace keeps us steady when everything feels chaotic. Faith is our shield against despair, salvation secures our hope, and God's Word is our sword—the only weapon that cuts through deception. We can't afford to go into our days unarmed.

3. Walking in Wisdom Without Fear

Trusting God doesn't mean being reckless. Proverbs 22:3 says, *"The prudent see danger and take refuge, but the simple keep going and pay the penalty."* There's a balance here. We lock our doors at night—not because we're afraid, but because wisdom says so. We prepare for emergencies—not with hoarding and panic, but with practical readiness. We avoid unnecessary risks—but we don't let fear stop us from sharing Jesus with our neighbors.

Think about Nehemiah's builders—they worked with a tool in one hand and a weapon in the other (Nehemiah 4:17). They trusted God *while* staying alert. That's our model. Faith and wisdom aren't opposites—they're partners.

4. Raising Kids Who Know Where Real Safety Is

Our kids are growing up in a world that's more unstable than ever. If we're not careful, they'll absorb the culture's fear and think security comes from money, approval, or control. But we get to show them something better.

When crises hit, we make prayer our *first* response—not our last resort. We tell them stories of God's faithfulness—how He shut the mouths of lions for Daniel, how He protected missionaries in impossible situations, how He's come through for *our* family again and again. We limit the fear-driven noise of the news and social media, replacing it with conversations about God's sovereignty. And we give them practical tools—like memorizing Psalm 91 together or talking through what to do in emergencies—so they're prepared but not paranoid.

Here's the bottom line: God's protection isn't about avoiding storms—it's about walking through them with Him. It's not a guarantee that nothing bad will ever happen; it's the promise that *nothing* can separate us from His love (Romans 8:38-39). So let's live like we believe it. Let's trust Him deeply, fight battles wisely, and pass that unshakable confidence to the next generation. Because in a world full of fear, God's people should be the most secure, steady, and hope-filled people on the planet.

Now—who's ready to live like that's true?

IV. Wrapping It Up: Your Unshakable Safe Place

Let's be real—life can feel pretty shaky sometimes, can't it? Between everything going on in the world and our own personal struggles, it's easy to feel like we're barely keeping it together. But here's the game-changer: Psalm 91 gives us this incredible picture of what it looks like to live *completely* safe in God.

That last verse hits different: *"Because he has set his love upon Me, therefore I will deliver him; I will set him on high, because he has known My name"* (v. 14). That's not just poetry—that's a rock-solid promise. As we head into each day, with all its unknowns, here's what we need to remember: If you're abiding in Jesus, you're safe. Not because bad things won't happen, but because *nothing* can touch you without passing through His hands first.

So what do we do with this? Here's your game plan for the year:

- **First, make Psalm 91 your anthem:** Memorize it. Pray it. When fear tries to creep in, speak it out loud. Let it become so woven into your heart that it's your automatic response when life feels out of control.

- **Second, do a daily "armor check.** Before you walk out the door or dive into your day, pause and ask: Am I grounded in truth today? Am I walking in integrity? Am I ready to share hope if someone needs it? Because here's the thing—spiritual battles are real, and we can't afford to go into our days unarmed.

- **Third, pick one area where fear's been messing with you**—maybe it's your health, your finances, or just the general chaos of the world—and flood it with Scripture. Every time that worry pops up, hit it with truth. Train your brain to default to trust instead of panic.

Here's the bottom line: God's protection doesn't mean we get a free pass from hard things. But it does mean that no matter what comes our way, **nothing**—not sickness, not financial stress, not even death itself—can rip us away from His love (Romans 8:38-39). The safest place in the universe isn't a bunker or a bank account—it's smack dab in the middle of God's will.

So let's live like we believe that. Let's be the people who walk through life with a peace that makes everyone around us wonder, "How are you so steady right now?" And when they ask—because they will—we'll get to tell them about the One who holds us secure.

Now that's how we face the future. Who's with me?

Chapter 5:

Peace – Christ's Unshakable Gift in a Troubled World

I. What Does the Bible Really Mean by Peace?

Let's talk about peace—not the Instagram-filtered version where everything looks perfect, but the *real*, unshakable peace the Bible describes. Because here's the thing: God's idea of peace is way bigger, way deeper, and way more powerful than just "no drama."

1. It's Way More Than "No Fighting"

In Hebrew, the word *shalom* isn't just about quiet moments or the absence of conflict. It's about *wholeness*—everything in your life, your relationships, and your soul being *exactly* as it should be. Think of it like a puzzle where every piece fits perfectly. That's *shalom*.

And in the New Testament, the Greek word *eirēnē* carries the same weight. When Jesus said, *"Peace I leave with you; My peace I give to you"* (John 14:27), He wasn't handing out a temporary calm. He was offering something *unbreakable*—a peace that doesn't just sit on the surface but goes bone-deep.

2. It Starts with Who You Know

Here's the game-changer: Biblical peace isn't something you create for yourself. It's not about meditation apps, vacation days, or avoiding conflict. It's about *reconciliation*—being brought back to God through Jesus.

Paul spells it out in Romans 5:1: *"Since we have been justified by faith, we have peace with God through our Lord Jesus Christ."* That's the foundation. Before we can experience peace *in* our lives, we need peace *with* God. And that only happens because of what Jesus did on the cross.

3. It Works Even When Life Doesn't

This is where it gets wild. The peace Jesus gives doesn't depend on your circumstances. Paul wrote about letting *"the peace of Christ rule in your hearts"* (Colossians 3:15) *while he was in prison,* waiting to possibly be executed. Let that sink in.

This peace isn't a fragile bubble that pops at the first sign of trouble. It's a *force*—something that *guards* your heart and mind (Philippians 4:7). Picture it like an armed security detail for your soul. When anxiety, fear, or chaos tries to break in, God's peace stands guard and says, *"Not today."*

4. It's Not Passive—It Rules

The word *"rule"* in Colossians 3:15 is actually an athletic term—it means to *umpire*, to call the shots. God's peace isn't just a nice feeling; it's meant to *govern* your decisions, your reactions, your entire life.

- When you're tempted to spiral into worry, peace says, *"God's got this."*
- When conflict tries to steal your joy, peace says, *"I'm anchored in something deeper."*
- When the world feels like it's falling apart, peace says, *"My future is secure in Christ."*

5. It's a Preview of Heaven

This peace isn't just for now—it's a taste of eternity. Isaiah called Jesus the *"Prince of Peace"* (Isaiah 9:6) because He's the one who will one day make *all things new*. No more brokenness. No more pain. Just perfect, complete *shalom*.

But until then? We get to live in *His* peace—a peace that doesn't make sense to the world, a peace that holds us steady when everything else is shaking.

So here's the bottom line: God's peace isn't about your circumstances. It's about *Him*. It's the kind of peace that doesn't just calm you—it *changes* you. And the best part? It's yours right now, no matter what's happening around you.

Who's ready to live like that's true?

II. Digging Deeper: What Does Real Peace Look Like?

Let's be honest—when we hear the word *peace*, we usually think of quiet moments, stress-free days, or the absence of conflict. But the Bible paints a *way* bigger picture. God's peace isn't just a feeling—it's a *reality* that changes everything.

A. God's Peace vs. the World's Knockoffs

Jesus said something revolutionary in John 14:27: *"My peace I give to you. Not as the world gives do I give to you."*

Think about that. The world's version of peace is *conditional*—it depends on everything going right.

- *Political peace?* It lasts until the next conflict.
- *Financial peace?* It disappears when the market crashes.
- *Personal peace?* It shatters when life gets hard.

But God's peace? It's *unshakable* because it's rooted in *Him*, not our circumstances. Colossians 1:20 says Jesus *"made peace through the blood of His cross."* That means real peace starts with *being right with God*.

And here's the crazy part—this peace doesn't just fix our relationship with God; it fixes our relationships with *each other*. Ephesians 2:14-15 says Jesus *"broke down the wall of hostility"* between Jews and Gentiles—two groups that *hated* each other. But in Christ? They became *family*.

That's the power of God's peace. It doesn't just *ignore* divisions—it *destroys* them. No government, no social movement, no self-help trend can do that. Only Jesus.

B. Peace in the Storm, Not After It

Here's where it gets wild. Jesus *promised* us trouble (John 16:33), but He also promised His peace *in the middle of it*.

Think about Paul and Silas in prison (Acts 16:25). Beaten. Locked up. Future uncertain. And what were they doing? *Singing*. Not because they were *happy* about their situation, but because they had a peace that *outlasted* their suffering.

Or Paul, writing *"Don't be anxious about anything"* (Philippians 4:6) *while chained to a Roman guard*. That's not denial—that's *supernatural* peace.

And this isn't just history—it's *our reality* in 2025. Following Jesus doesn't mean life gets *easier*; it means we get *steadier*. When the world panics, we have an anchor. When culture shifts, we have a foundation.

This peace isn't about pretending everything's fine. It's about knowing *God's in control* even when *nothing* makes sense.

C. Fake Peace vs. the Real Thing

Let's be real—we live in a world *desperate* for peace, but most of what's out there is a cheap imitation.

- *Political utopias?* They promise peace through control, but ignore human sin.
- *Mindfulness & meditation?* They might calm your mind, but can't fix your soul.
- *Entertainment & distractions?* They numb the pain, but don't heal it.
- *Substance abuse?* It's a temporary escape with permanent consequences.
- *Religious rituals?* They can become empty habits if they're not about *knowing Jesus*.

All these counterfeits have one thing in common: **They're *temporary*. They work—until they don't.**

But Christ's peace? It's *different.*

- It's *lasting*—because it's based on His finished work.
- It's *deep*—because it changes us from the inside out.
- It's *unshakable*—because it doesn't depend on our situation.

Isaiah 48:22 says it straight: *"There is no peace for the wicked."* Real peace only comes through *surrender to Christ.*

The Bottom Line

God's peace isn't about avoiding storms—it's about *who's in the boat with you.* It's not a *feeling*; it's a *person*—Jesus. And when we have *Him*, we have everything we need.

So let me ask you: *Which peace are you living in?* **The world's flimsy substitute—or the real, unbreakable, Jesus-given kind?**

III. Living Out God's Peace in Everyday Life

Let's get practical—how do we actually *live* in this unshakable peace Jesus promised? It's not just a nice idea—it's something we can build into our daily rhythms, even in the chaos of 2024.

1. Personal Peace: It Starts with Your Walk with God

Peace isn't automatic—it's cultivated. Think of it like a garden. If you don't tend to it, weeds of worry and fear will take over.

- **Feed your mind on Scripture.** Pick a few key verses (like Isaiah 26:3 or Philippians 4:6-7) and *marinate* on them. Write them on sticky notes, set them as phone reminders—let them reshape how you think.
- **Pray like it's a conversation, not a wish list.** Try the ACTS method: Start by *worshiping* God for who He is, then *confess* anything blocking your connection with Him, *thank* Him for specific blessings, and *then* bring your requests.
- **Keep a "peace journal."** Write down moments when God came through for you. When anxiety hits, flip through it and remind yourself: *"He was faithful then—He'll be faithful now."*

2. Relational Peace: Being a Peacemaker in a Divided World

Let's be real—relationships can be messy. But Jesus called us to be *peacemakers* (Matthew 5:9), not just peacekeepers.

- **In marriage/family:** Set up a weekly "peace check-in." No phones, no distractions—just honest conversation. When you mess up (and you will), *own it.* Say, *"I was wrong. Will you forgive me?"* That models Christlike humility for your kids.
- **In conflict:** Use the *"3D Approach"*—*Discern* (is this battle worth fighting?), *Dialogue* (ask questions before making statements), and *Disengage* if things turn toxic (but leave the door open for reconciliation).
- **Online:** Before firing off that heated reply, *wait 24 hours.* Pray first. Maybe God will lead you to respond—or maybe He'll show you that silence is stronger.

3. Emotional Peace: Staying Steady in a Chaotic World

The news cycle is designed to keep us anxious. But we don't have to live that way.

- **Set boundaries with media.** Maybe 30 minutes of news in the morning and evening—then *pray* over what you've heard. Swap doom-scrolling for a walk outside or serving someone in need.
- **Take care of your body.** It's hard to feel at peace when you're exhausted or running on caffeine and junk food. Move your body. Eat foods that fuel your brain (like salmon, nuts, leafy greens).
  - **Sleep like it's spiritual.** If anxiety keeps you up, create a wind-down routine: No screens before bed. Sip herbal tea. Listen to Scripture or worship music. Let God's Word be the last thing on your mind.

4. Passing Peace to the Next Generation

Our kids are growing up in a world that feeds them fear. We have to *show* them what real peace looks like.

- **Make faith tangible.** Create a "peace wall" at home—answered prayers, encouraging verses, reminders of God's faithfulness. Talk about it often.

- **Give them tools.** Teach little ones simple breathing prayers (*"Breathe in God's peace, breathe out worries"*). Give pre-teens a journal to record answered prayers. Equip teens with a "panic verse" (like Isaiah 41:10) for their wallet.

- **Role-play real life.** Practice stressful scenarios: *"What if someone bullies you?" "What if you hear scary news?"* Coach them to respond with truth, not fear.

- **Most importantly—model it.** When stress hits, *say out loud*: *"This is hard, but God's got us."* Kids remember what they *see* more than what they *hear*.

Bottom Line: God's peace isn't about pretending life is perfect. It's about knowing *the Prince of Peace* walks with us through the mess. The world's version of peace is flimsy—here today, gone tomorrow. But *His* peace? That's the real deal.

So let's live like it. One day, one choice, one prayer at a time. Who's in?

IV. Wrapping It Up: Peace That Wins

Let's be real—Our world isn't going to be a walk in the park. Between the chaos in the news, the pressures of daily life, and the constant noise of the world, it's easy to feel like peace is just a nice idea that doesn't stand a chance. But here's the truth: Jesus' peace isn't just a feeling—it's a force.

This peace rules in our hearts (Colossians 3:15)—not like a gentle suggestion, but like an umpire calling the shots. It doesn't mean we ignore reality; it means we face reality from the unshakable place of being in Christ. Isaiah 26:3 says God keeps us in perfect peace when our minds are stayed on Him—not on our fears, not on the news, not on the worst-case scenarios. That's a game-changer.

So what do we do with this? Here's your game plan for the year:

- **Make Psalm 91 Your Battle Song** This psalm is like a spiritual shield. Memorize it. Pray it out loud when fear tries to creep in. Let it be your go-to when the world feels out of control.

- **Suit Up Every. Single. Day.** Before you walk out the door (or even check your phone), do a quick armor check (Ephesians 6:10-18). Truth buckled around your waist. Righteousness guarding your heart. Gospel peace on your feet. Faith as your shield. Salvation securing your mind. God's Word in your hand, ready to fight lies with truth. Don't leave home unarmed.

- **Take Down Fear Strongholds** We all have that one area where anxiety loves to camp out—money, health, family, the future. Identify yours, then flood it with Scripture. Write down promises that speak directly to that fear and declare them daily. Fear can't stand when truth moves in.

Here's the bottom line: Jesus' peace has already overcome the world (John 16:33). That means no storm, no crisis, no uncertainty can wreck what He's built in you. When we live in that peace—really live in it—we become walking proof that Christ's power shines brightest in our weakness (2 Corinthians 12:9).

So let's step into tomorrow with a peace that doesn't just survive the chaos but stands out in it. Let's live so rooted in Jesus that people can't help but ask, **"How are you so steady right now?"**

And when they do? We'll point them to the Prince of Peace. Now that's a win.

Chapter 6:

Promise – The Certainty of God's Word in an Uncertain World

I. What Does the Bible Really Mean by "Promise"?

Let's talk about promises—not the kind we casually make and break ("Yeah, I'll call you tomorrow"), but the kind that actually *mean* something. When the Bible talks about God's promises, it's not just wishful thinking or optimistic small talk. It's rock-solid, unshakable, *covenant-level* commitment from the One who *cannot* lie (Titus 1:2).

Think about it like this: Human promises are flimsy. We say things like, "I promise I'll be there," and then traffic happens, or we forget, or we just change our minds. But God's promises? They're backed by His *entire character*—His power, His knowledge, His unchanging nature. From His covenant with Noah (Genesis 9:11) to His guarantee of eternal life through Jesus (1 John 2:25), every promise is a sacred bond, not just a nice sentiment.

Here's what makes God's promises different:

1. **They're rooted in *who He is*, not circumstances.** Human promises depend on things staying the same—no surprises, no unexpected bills, no sudden changes of heart. But God's promises don't wobble when life gets messy. Why? Because He's the same yesterday, today, and forever (Hebrews 13:8). Culture shifts, governments rise and fall, and we might waver—but His word *doesn't*.

2. **They're sealed with *double certainty*. W**hen God made His promise to Abraham, He didn't just say, "Cross my heart." Hebrews 6:18 tells us He backed it with an *oath*—two unchangeable things (His word *and* His oath) because, for Him, it's *impossible* to lie. That's like signing a contract in permanent ink, then welding it shut.

3. **They unfold on *His timeline*, not ours.** Some of God's promises took *centuries* to fully play out. Abraham didn't live to see the whole story (hello, Messiah!), but that didn't make the promise any less real. Fast-forward to today, and we're *still* benefiting from what God swore to him (Galatians 3:16). That's the thing about divine promises—they're bigger than our lifespan, our understanding, or our impatience.

So when you're in a season of waiting, when prayers feel unanswered, or when the world seems to be falling apart, here's the truth to cling to: **God's promises don't expire, don't fail, and don't rely on human cooperation to come true.** They're as steady as He is.

And that changes everything.

II. Digging Deeper: What Makes God's Promises So Different?

Let's be honest—we've all been burned by broken promises. Maybe a friend flaked on plans, or a job offer fell through, or someone swore they'd change... but didn't. Human promises often crumble under pressure. But God's promises? They're in a league of their own. Here's why:

A. God's Promises Are Covenant, Not Contracts

When God makes a promise, it's not some casual pinky swear. It's a *covenant*—a sacred, unbreakable bond. Take Abraham: God showed up and said, *"I'm giving you land, descendants like the stars, and through you, the whole world will be blessed"* (Genesis 12:1-3, 15:5). No negotiations. No fine print. Just *"I'm doing this because I said I would."*

And here's the kicker: **God's covenants don't depend on us.** Human contracts fall apart when one side drops the ball. But God's promises? They rest entirely on *His* faithfulness. Even when Abraham tried to "help" God by having a son with Hagar (Genesis 16), God didn't cancel the plan. He kept His word—on His terms, in His time.

Fast-forward to Jesus, and we see the ultimate fulfillment: *"All God's promises find their 'Yes' in Him"* (2 Corinthians 1:20). The New Covenant (Jeremiah 31:31-34) wasn't about rules but *relationship*—God writing His law on our hearts, wiping our slate clean, and calling us His own. And He sealed it with blood—not Abraham's, not ours, but *Christ's* (Luke 22:20).

So what does this mean for us?

God's promises aren't lottery tickets to scratch off for quick wins. They're part of His grand rescue plan. When we feel stuck waiting, it helps to remember: His timing isn't slow—it's *strategic*.

B. The Waiting Room of Faith

Let's talk about the elephant in the room: **Why do God's promises often take so long?**

Abraham waited *25 years* for Isaac. Joseph's dreams of leadership led to a *13-year detour* through slavery and prison. Israel groaned for centuries under foreign rulers, begging, *"How long, Lord?"* (Habakkuk 1:2). Even Jesus' arrival was perfectly timed—*"when the fullness of time had come"* (Galatians 4:4).

Here's the truth we hate but need: **Delay isn't denial.** God uses waiting to:

- Strip away our half-baked faith (like Abraham learning to trust God's plan, not his own).
- Expose the idols we cling to for security (like Joseph's pride in those early dreams).
- Teach us to depend on *Him,* not just the outcome we're begging for.

Waiting isn't God forgetting His promises—it's Him *preparing us* to handle them well.

C. Fake Promises vs. the Real Deal

Our world is full of knockoff "promises" that crash and burn:

- **Prosperity gospel:** *"Follow God, and you'll get rich!"* (Meanwhile, Paul was shipwrecked and starving.)
- **Self-help hype:** *"Believe in yourself!"* (Cool, until you face death, sin, or a broken world.)
- **Political utopias:** Every generation thinks *their* system will fix everything. (Spoiler: None do.)

Even in church circles, we twist promises. We treat verses like magic spells—*"Claim it!"*—while ignoring that some promises come with conditions (*"If you abide in Me..."* John 15:7) or unfold in ways we'd never expect (*"My thoughts are not your thoughts..."* Isaiah 55:8). **Real faith holds promises with open hands.** We trust God's wisdom in *how* and *when* He fulfills them—even if some wait until eternity (Hebrews 11:39-40).

Bottom Line: God's promises aren't just nice words. They're unshakable truths anchored in His character. The next time you're tempted to doubt, remember: **If He said it, He'll do it.** Maybe not how you pictured. Maybe not when you wanted. But always—*always*—in the way that's best. GOD IS NEVER LATE

Now *that's* a promise worth building your life on.

III. Living Out God's Promises in Real Time

Let's get real—knowing *about* God's promises is one thing, but actually *building your life on them*? That's where things get practical (and honestly, where most of us struggle). Here's how to move from theory to everyday faith.

1. Making God's Promises Your Foundation

You wouldn't build a house on sand, right? The same goes for your faith. God's promises are the bedrock, but we've got to *engage* with them, not just nod along on Sundays.

Start here:

- **Sort the promises.** Not all work the same way. Some are *unconditional* (God says, "I'll do this no matter what"—like *"I'll never leave you"* [Hebrews 13:5]). Others are *conditional* (*"If you confess, I'll forgive"* [1 John 1:9]). And some are *future-focused* (Jesus *will* return [John 14:3]).

- **Keep a "promise journal."** Organize verses by what you're facing—fear, finances, guidance—and add notes when God comes through. Over time, you'll see patterns: *"Oh, this is how He works."*

- **Memorize strategically.** When anxiety hits, you want Philippians 4:6-7 ready to go. Stash verses where you'll see them—on your mirror, in your car, as your phone lock screen. For families, make it a game: *"How did David use God's promises when facing Goliath?"*

Why this matters: Life's storms *will* come. But when you've hidden God's promises in your heart, you won't drown in the "what-ifs."

2. When God Says "Wait" (And It's Taking Forever)

Let's be honest—waiting stinks. Whether it's a prodigal child, a health battle, or a dream that seems stuck, unfulfilled promises can make us doubt. But here's the thing: **Delay isn't denial.**

What to do when you're stuck in the "middle":

- **Avoid Saul's mistake.** He panicked when God seemed slow and took matters into his own hands (1 Samuel 13). Don't force what God hasn't authorized.

- **But don't just sit there.** Biblical waiting is *active*—like a farmer planting seeds *while* trusting God for rain (James 5:7). Pray for your prodigal, but also love them like Jesus would. Claim healing, but also learn from Paul's thorn: sometimes God's *"My grace is enough"* (2 Corinthians 12:9) is the greater gift.

- **Study the "waiters."** Joseph's prison time prepped him to save nations. David protected the king who was trying to kill him because he trusted God's timing (1 Samuel 24). Their stories remind us: **God's pauses have purpose.**

For your church: Create a "faithfulness wall" where people post stories of God showing up *after* long waits. Nothing fuels hope like seeing others cross the finish line.

3. Spotting Fake Promises (Because the World's Full of Them)

From *"Name it and claim it!"* to *"Follow your heart,"* our culture peddles empty slogans. Here's how to tell the real from the rip-off: **Red flags:**

- **The prosperity trap:** If a preacher says, *"Just believe, and you'll get rich!"* but never mentions suffering (2 Corinthians 11:23-28) or sacrifice (Mark 10:28-30), run.
- **The "feel-good" counterfeit:** *"You create your reality!"* sounds empowering—until crisis hits. Compare everything to Scripture. God's promises don't ignore pain; they *redeem* it.
- **The "guaranteed outcome" lie:** Some treat promises like vending machines (*"Insert prayer, receive miracle"*). But even Jesus prayed, *"Your will be done"* (Matthew 26:39).

Safeguards:
- **Check the fine print.** Many promises come with conditions (*"If you abide in Me..."* [John 15:7]).
- **Balance the Bible.** Yes, God heals (Matthew 8), but Paul's thorn (2 Corinthians 12) shows He sometimes permits weakness for greater purposes.
- **Teach kids early.** Use social media posts to discuss: *"This influencer says 'believe in yourself'—what does God say?"* (Jeremiah 17:9).

4. Showing the World What Real Hope Looks Like

In a culture of broken trust (politicians lie, brands scam, relationships crumble), *unshakable* faith stands out.

How to shine:
- **Tell your story.** Nothing disarms skeptics like *"Here's how God held me when..."*—whether it's cancer, job loss, or addiction recovery.

- **Create "promise walls."** Let your church display answered prayers with the verses that anchored people. *"This is how God provided when we had no money."*
- **Engage doubts honestly.** When skeptics ask, *"Why doesn't God answer?"* admit: *"Sometimes I wonder too. But here's why I still trust Him..."* Point to the resurrection (1 Corinthians 15:20)—proof that *no* promise will fail.

Bottom Line: God's promises aren't just ancient words. They're *alive*. They've held up through centuries, through crises, through our worst moments. And in 2075? They'll still be standing.

So plant your life on them. When the world wobbles, you won't.

IV. Wrapping It Up: Where to Stand When Everything Feels Shaky

Let's not kid ourselves—the life isn't going to be a walk in the park. Markets will wobble. News headlines will scream chaos. People will keep letting us down. But here's the game-changer: **God's promises don't have an expiration date.** They're not tied to the stock market, election cycles, or cultural moods. As Peter put it, *"The word of the Lord endures forever"* (1 Peter 1:25). That means what God said centuries ago to Abraham, David, and Paul still holds up today—and every single promise points back to Jesus (2 Corinthians 1:20).

Some promises hit fast. Some take a lifetime to unfold. Some we won't see fully until eternity. But here's what we know for sure: **If God said it, it's as good as done.**

Your Game Plan Starting Tomorrow

1. **Take the "100 Promises Challenge"** Each week, pick one promise to memorize—not just the verse, but the *story* behind

it. Keep a journal: *"This is how I saw God come through this month."* Pro tip: Start with the promises that address what keeps you up at night.

2. **Find Your Promise Partner** Team up with someone further along in faith (or someone you can encourage). Meet monthly to say: *"Where are you struggling to trust God's timing? Let's pray through that."* This isn't about fixing each other—it's about reminding each other *"He's still faithful."*

3. **Throw a Testimony Party (Yes, Really)** Every few months, gather friends to share *"Here's how God showed up."* No sanitized stories allowed—real struggles, real breakthroughs. These nights are rocket fuel for faith when doubts creep in.

Why This Matters

When we live like this, we're not just *believing* God's promises—we're *proving* them. In a world of empty slogans and broken contracts, that kind of consistency shouts louder than any sermon.

So here's to **LIFE**—not because it'll be easy, but because **we know the One who's already written the last chapter.** Let's live like we trust Him.

Who's in?

Chapter 7:

Power – The Demonstration of God's Strength in Human Weakness

I. What the Bible Really Means by "Power"

Let's cut through the noise—when the world talks about power, it's usually about who's got the most money, the biggest army, or the loudest voice. But God? He flips the script entirely.

The Bible shows us that power isn't about flexing strength or forcing control. Real power—*God's* power—is about *holy energy* that flows from His very nature to get His perfect will done. Think of it like this: Jesus didn't do miracles to show off. When He shut down storms with a word (Mark 4:39) or healed a woman who'd been sick for decades (Luke 8:43-48), it wasn't magic tricks—it was *redemption in action*. Even the resurrection wasn't just a comeback story—it was God's power obliterating death itself (Romans 1:4).

Here's what makes divine power *so* different:

- **It doesn't run on our fuel.** Human power depends on stuff that fades—money, influence, and physical strength. But God's power comes from *who He is*—eternal, unshakable, and completely self-sufficient (Psalm 62:11).

- **It thrives in our weakness.** Sounds backward, right? But Paul nailed it: *"When I am weak, then I am strong"* (2 Corinthians 12:10). God's power doesn't just *help* us—it *shows up best* when we're out of our depth, because that's when we stop pretending we've got it all together.

- **It rewrites the rules.** The cross should've been a symbol of defeat. Instead, God turned it into the ultimate display of power—breaking sin's grip and death's hold (1 Corinthians 1:18). That's the kind of power that doesn't play by the world's playbook.

So here's the takeaway: God's power isn't about making *us* look good. It's about *His* glory, *His* purpose, and *His* unstoppable plan. And the crazy part? **He lets us in on it—not because we're strong enough, but because *He* is.**

II. Breaking Down God's Power: It's Not What You Think

Let's get real about power—because God's version turns everything we know upside down.

A. God's Power: The Real Deal

God's power isn't something He turns on and off—it's *who He is*. The fancy word is **omnipotence**, meaning He can do *anything* that fits His perfect nature (Jeremiah 32:17). This isn't theoretical—we see it in action when He:

- Spoke the universe into existence (Genesis 1:3)
- Ripped Israel out of Egypt's grip (Exodus 14:31)
- Turned the cross—a symbol of defeat—into Satan's worst nightmare (Colossians 2:15)

Unlike us (who get tired, hit limits, or lose steam), God's power *never* fades (Isaiah 40:28). But here's what's wild: His power *always* plays nice with His other traits. It's fueled by love (Ephesians 3:17-19), guided by wisdom (Romans 11:33), and kept in check by justice (Psalm 89:14). That's why He'll never abuse it or act randomly.

The cross proves it. What looked like Jesus' weakest moment? That was actually God's power on full display—breaking sin's back through what seemed like defeat (Philippians 2:5-8). His ways *will* mess with your head (Isaiah 55:8-9), but they *always* work.

B. Weakness = God's Power Playground

Here's the Bible's most counterintuitive idea: *Your weakness is God's favorite place to work.* Paul begged God to remove his "thorn" (some chronic pain or struggle), but God said, *"Nope—My power works best in weakness"* (2 Corinthians 12:9).

Jesus modeled this, too. He didn't flex divine muscle 24/7 but said, *"I only do what I see the Father doing"* (John 5:19). The early church got it—when persecution scattered them (human failure?), the gospel *exploded* (Acts 8:4).

For us? That means:

- **Your chronic illness? A stage for His power.**
- **Your empty bank account? His provision of opportunity.**
- **Your broken relationships? His redemption project.**

Stop hiding your weaknesses. Like Paul, *lean into them*—because that's where Jesus shows up strongest.

C. Fake Power Alert

The world peddles cheap substitutes:

- *Political power?* **Can't fix human hearts (Jeremiah 17:9).**
- *Money?* **Vanishes faster than Bitcoin (Proverbs 23:5).**
- *Occult stuff?* **Straight-up bondage (Acts 19:19).**

Even in church circles, we've got counterfeits:

- *Revival hype* **without lasting change**
- ***"Name it and claim it"* theology that ignores suffering**

Real power? It:

- **Aligns with Scripture (1 John 4:1)**
- **Grows fruit like love and patience (Galatians 5:22-23)**
- **Works in quiet faithfulness (Colossians 3:23)** *and miracles*

Test everything. Because even Satan masquerades as light (2 Corinthians 11:14)—but God's power *always* points back to Jesus.

Bottom Line: God's power doesn't look like the world's. It's *better*—and it's yours when you stop pretending you've got it all together.

III. Putting God's Power to Work Tomorrow

Let's get practical—how do we actually *live* in God's power when life feels overwhelming? It's not about waiting for lightning bolts from heaven. Real spiritual power flows from daily habits, surrendered weakness, and ordinary moments where we let God work through us.

1. Power Habits: More Than Just a Morning Routine

God's power isn't a one-time zap—it's fuel for the long haul. Start your day with a simple prayer like Psalm 28:7: *"Lord, You're my strength—I'm leaning on You today."* That mindset shift alone changes everything.

Want ammunition for tough moments? **Hide Scripture in your heart.** When fear hits, Isaiah 41:10 (*"Fear not, I'm with you"*) is your go-to. When you're drained, Isaiah 40:31 (*"He'll renew your strength"*) becomes your lifeline. Write these verses where you'll see them—on your bathroom mirror, in your car, even as your phone wallpaper.

Try fasting—but keep it real. Skip lunch once a month and use that time to pray instead. Feeling extra bold? Do a 3-day fast (with your pastor's guidance and plenty of water!). Hunger pangs become prayer prompts—every growling stomach is a reminder: *"God, I need You more than food."*

And don't sleep on **corporate worship.** When believers unite in praise, chains break (Acts 16:25-26). Show up to church expecting God to move—sing like you mean it, pray boldly for others, and watch what happens.

2. Spiritual Authority: Not a Superpower, But Close

Jesus gave every believer real authority (Luke 10:19)—but it's not about bossing demons around like a Hollywood exorcist.

- **Pray with boldness *and* humility.** Command mountains to move (Mark 11:23), but also say, *"Your will be done"* (1 John 5:14). Pray for healing, but trust God whether He zaps the sickness away, guides doctors, or gives grace to endure.

- **Facing darkness? Keep it simple.** If you sense spiritual oppression, speak Psalm 91 out loud, pray for light to flood the space, and don't get into debates with demons. For serious cases, call in mature believers—this isn't a solo mission.

- **Leaders, check your motives.** Power corrupts when unchecked. No guilt-tripping people into giving. No controlling others' lives. Build accountability—because the enemy loves to hijack God's authority for selfish agendas.

3. Power in the Everyday Grind

God's not waiting for you to become a preacher to use you. Some of the most powerful ministry happens in cubicles, school pick-up lines, and your Instagram DMs.

- **At work:** Be the person who won't cut corners (like Daniel refusing the king's food). When coworkers vent, pray for them silently—then watch for chances to say, *"Hey, can I tell you how God helped me through something similar?"*

- **At home:** Break generational junk. If anger, addiction, or occult stuff runs in your family, repent of it aloud (*"This stops with me"*). Fill your house with Scripture—stick verses on fridge doors, play audio Bibles in the background.

- **Online:** Skip the political mudslinging. Instead, post *"Here's how God showed up when I was jobless/heartbroken/broke."* Real stories disarm skeptics faster than theological mic drops.

- **In crisis:** Rally prayer warriors. Facing a diagnosis or legal battle? Text friends: *"Let's agree in prayer this week."* Keep a record—when God answers, it becomes fuel for future faith.

4. Raising a Power-Filled Next Gen

Kids aren't just the church of tomorrow—they're warriors *today*. Here's how to equip them:

- **Teach them to pray like it matters.** At bedtime, pray simple, expectant prayers together (*"God, heal Sarah's scraped knee!"*). Share stories of when God answered *your* prayers.

- **Warning label:** The occult isn't harmless. Explain why horoscopes, Ouija boards, and "psychic" games are dangerous (Deuteronomy 18:10-12). No scare tactics—just truth: *"This stuff opens doors to real darkness."*

- **Model power under control.** When you lose your temper, apologize (*"I was wrong to yell. Will you forgive me?"*). Kids learn that true strength isn't about volume—it's about self-control.
- **Create "power labs."** Let teens practice praying for headaches or minor injuries. Debrief afterward: *"What did you sense God saying? What felt off?"* Normalize hearing God's voice.

Bottom Line: God's power isn't reserved for super-Christians. It's for *you*—in your weaknesses, your mundane moments, your messes. Tomorrow might be chaotic, but you're armed with something unshakable.

Now go live like it.

IV. Wrapping It Up: Why God's Power Changes Everything

\# **Real Talk**—the world's getting crazier by the minute. Fake miracles, empty promises, and spiritual counterfeits are everywhere (2 Thessalonians 2:9-12). But here's the game-changer: The same power that raised Jesus out of the grave is alive in you right now (Ephesians 1:19-20).

This isn't just theory—it's explosive, life-altering reality. And get this: It's not just for pastors or "super-spiritual" people. It's for anyone willing to admit, "I can't do this alone—I need You, God."

Action Steps Starting Tomorrow:

1. **Conduct a "Power Audit"**—Journal areas where you rely on self (finances, relationships, ministry) rather than the Spirit. Repent of self-sufficiency and ask for fresh filling (Ephesians 5:18).

2. **Launch a "Power Prayer Initiative"**—Gather believers weekly to pray for revival in specific societal spheres (government, education, media). Research needs and claim relevant Scriptures.

3. **Study Acts Devotionally**—Note how the early church accessed power through prayer (Acts 4:23-31), unity (Acts 2:44), and bold witness (Acts 4:20). Apply one principle weekly.

Bottom Line: The world's running on empty promises. But you? You're wired to the ultimate power source. Now live like it and show others, too.

Chapter 8:

Perseverance – Remaining Steadfast in Faith Despite Hardships

I. What Does the Bible Really Mean by Perseverance?

Let's cut through the noise—when the Bible talks about perseverance, it's not just about gritting your teeth and toughing it out. This isn't some motivational "don't quit" speech. Biblical perseverance (*hypomonē* in Greek) is something deeper, richer, and way more powerful than sheer human stubbornness.

1. It's Not Just "Hanging On"

Perseverance in Scripture isn't passive survival mode. It's *active, Spirit-fueled endurance*—the kind that keeps going when everything in you wants to bail. Jesus didn't mince words: *"The one who endures to the end will be saved"* (Matthew 10:22). Notice He didn't say *"the one who starts strong"* or *"the one who has it all together."* Endurance is non-negotiable for real faith.

The apostles painted vivid pictures of what this looks like:

- **Marathon Runner (Hebrews 12:1):** The Christian life isn't a sprint; it's a grueling, long-distance race where endurance matters more than speed. Just as runners shed unnecessary weight, we must ditch sin and distractions that trip us up. The crowd of faithful believers who've gone before us (Hebrews 11) cheers us on—their lives prove it's possible to finish strong.

- **Soldier (2 Timothy 2:3-4):** Spiritual warfare requires single-minded focus. Soldiers don't get entangled in civilian affairs—they stay mission-ready. For us, this means refusing to let comfort, entertainment, or fear distract us from God's calling. The battle's real, but so is our Commander's presence.

- **Farmer (James 5:7-8):** Crops don't grow overnight. Farmers labor through droughts, storms, and waiting seasons because they trust the harvest is coming. Our perseverance plants gospel seeds that will yield eternal fruit—even when we can't yet see results.

2. It's Rooted in Who God Is

Here's the game-changer: **We can persevere because God *first* persevered with us.** The Bible describes Him as *"slow to anger and abounding in steadfast love"* (Exodus 34:6). Translation? God doesn't give up on us—ever.

- **God's Track Record:** From Genesis to Revelation, God sticks with rebellious Israel, wayward prophets, and flawed disciples. His patience with Peter's denials, Elijah's burnout, and Jonah's rebellion proves His commitment isn't based on our performance.

- **Jesus' Example (Hebrews 12:2-3):** Christ endured the cross—betrayal, torture, and divine abandonment—for the joy of redeeming us. When we're tempted to quit, we fix our eyes on Him. His resurrection guarantees our struggles aren't pointless.

3. It's a Supernatural Gift, Not a Self-Help Hack

Let's be real—you can't white-knuckle your way through real trials on willpower alone. Biblical perseverance isn't about *"just try harder."* It's about leaning into the Spirit's strength when yours is gone.

- **Grace Sustains Us (1 Peter 1:5; Jude 24):** Our endurance isn't self-generated; it's *"God who guards and keeps us"* (Jude 24, AMP). Like a parent teaching a child to walk while holding their hands, the Holy Spirit upholds us even when we stumble.

- **Paul's Testimony (Philippians 4:13):** Written from prison, this verse isn't a prosperity slogan. It's raw testimony: *"I've faced starvation, beatings, and shipwrecks. Yet through Christ's power, I'm still standing."* His secret? Dependency, not dominance.

- **Daily Bread Principle:** Just as Israel relied on *daily* manna (Exodus 16), perseverance is nurtured through *daily* communion with God. Bible meditation, prayer, and fellowship aren't religious duties—they're survival tactics.

Bottom Line: Perseverance isn't optional. It's the mark of real faith. But here's the good news: **You don't have to manufacture it.** God's faithfulness fuels yours. So when you hit the wall (and you will), remember—you're not running this race alone.

Now *that's* endurance that lasts.

II. The Beautiful Tension of Perseverance: God's Work and Our Walk

Let's talk about one of the most mind-blowing truths in Scripture - how God's unshakable grip on us somehow doesn't cancel out our real responsibility to keep following Him. This isn't some theological contradiction; it's the beautiful dance of grace in action.

A. The Divine-Human Partnership

Here's the paradox: God promises He'll never let go of His people (John 10:28-29), yet commands us to "fight the good fight of faith" (1

Timothy 6:12). Both are gloriously true. It's like how Ezekiel 36:27 says God puts His Spirit in us to make us obey - yet Philippians 2:12 tells us to "work out your salvation with fear and trembling."

This isn't some theological loophole - it's the heartbeat of a covenant relationship. God starts the work, powers the work, and finishes the work (Philippians 1:6), but we're not passive puppets. The Westminster Confession puts it perfectly: "Those God saves can't totally fall away... but yes, they'll still mess up and need to repent."

Three passages show this partnership in action:

In **Philippians 2:12-13**, Paul gives us that famous "work out your salvation... because God works in you" tension. The Greek here is brilliant - "work out" means bringing something to completion, while "works" refers to God's energy fueling us. It's like a child learning to ride a bike while their parent steadies them.

Peter shows the same balance in **2 Peter 1:3-11** - God gives everything we need for godliness, then says "make every effort" to live it out. It's like being handed a fully stocked toolbox - the tools are free, but we've got to use them.

And Paul's testimony in **1 Corinthians 15:10** nails it: "I worked harder than anyone!" followed immediately by "but actually, it was God's grace working through me." His sweat was real, but the power wasn't his own.

B. Two Ditches to Avoid

First, there's complacency - thinking "God's got me, so I can coast." That's what Jude 4 calls turning grace into a license to sin. But God's preservation isn't a backstage pass to ignore holiness.

Then there's anxiety - the fear that "if I mess up, I'm out." Jesus didn't say "Strive until you collapse" but "Come to me... and I'll give you rest" (Matthew 11:28-30).

Peter's story shows the perfect balance: Jesus told him, "I've prayed your faith won't fail" (divine preservation). Yet after denying Christ, Peter still had to "turn back" (human responsibility) (Luke 22:32). Both were true.

C. What This Means for Us Today

We can have rock-solid assurance in Christ (Hebrews 12:2) while passionately pursuing holiness (Hebrews 12:14). We're called to vigorous effort (Colossians 1:29), but not in our own strength - like a sailboat harnessing wind power instead of rowing frantically.

And our spiritual disciplines? They're not boxes to check to earn God's love, but lifelines plugging us into grace that's already ours.

Bottom Line: Our perseverance is 100% God's work - and 100% our fight. The tension isn't a problem to solve but a mystery to live in. Christ started this work in you, and He'll finish it (Philippians 1:6) - so keep running, knowing His grip on you is tighter than your grip on Him.

D. Why Trials Matter: God's Refining Fire

Let's get real about suffering - because the Bible doesn't treat it as God's absence but as His refining fire. James 1:2-4 shocks us by saying to "count it all joy" when trials come, because they produce steadfast endurance. This isn't about enjoying pain, but recognizing its purpose.

The early church got this - they actually rejoiced when persecuted (Acts 5:41), not because they were masochists, but because they saw suffering as sharing in Christ's mission (Colossians 1:24). Their secret? Knowing present troubles were working an "eternal weight of glory" (2 Corinthians 4:17).

Case Studies in Faith Under Fire:

Job shows us how to lament honestly while holding onto faith. God didn't explain his suffering but revealed Himself more deeply (Job 38-42).

Joseph's betrayal and prison time weren't detours but preparation for saving nations (Genesis 50:20).

And Paul's "thorn in the flesh" (2 Corinthians 12:7-10) proves God sometimes sustains us in struggles rather than removing them, keeping us dependent on grace.

Three Types of Suffering Scripture Identifies:

1. **Punitive suffering from sin (1 Peter 4:15) - requiring repentance**
2. **Sanctifying suffering - God's loving discipline (Hebrews 12:5-11)**
3. **Missional suffering - persecution for Christ (Philippians 1:29)**

This keeps us from either fatalism ("all pain is meaningless") or escapism ("faith means no troubles").

Four Pillars of a Biblical View of Suffering:

1. **God is sovereign over every trial (Job 1-2)**
2. **He wastes no pain in His plan (Romans 8:28)**
3. **Present suffering prepares eternal glory (2 Corinthians 4:17)**
4. **Our pain equips us to comfort others (2 Corinthians 1:3-4)**

These aren't just abstract ideas - they're lifelines I've clung to in my own darkest moments.

First, God's sovereignty in our suffering. When we read Job's story, it's easy to focus on his losses - his health, wealth, even his children. But the real shocker comes in the first two chapters, where we see God actually initiating the conversation about Job with Satan. This isn't a distant God unaware of our pain - this is a God so thoroughly in control that even Satan can't touch us without permission. That changes everything when we're in the hospital room or the unemployment line. The trials we face aren't random chaos breaking through God's defenses - they're permitted by a Father who knows exactly what He's doing, even when we don't.

Then there's Romans 8:28 - that famous promise that God works all things for good. But we often miss the context. This isn't some trite "everything happens for a reason" platitude. It's sandwiched between Paul talking about the Spirit's groaning intercession (v.26) and the unshakable love of Christ (v.35). The "good" here isn't about our temporary comfort - it's about being conformed to Christ's image (v.29). I've seen this in my own life - the most painful seasons became the crucible where God burned away my self-reliance and taught me to lean on Him. He doesn't waste our pain any more than a master chef wastes ingredients - every bitter experience gets redeemed in His hands.

2 Corinthians 4:17 hits even harder. Paul calls our present sufferings "light and momentary" - which feels laughable when you're in the thick of grief or chronic pain. But he's comparing them to an "eternal weight of glory" that makes our worst days on earth seem insignificant in the grand scheme. It's like comparing a papercut to winning the Nobel Prize. This perspective shift changes how we endure - not by minimizing our pain, but by maximizing our view of what's coming. The suffering isn't pointless - it's actually producing something of eternal value in us.

Finally, 2 Corinthians 1:3-4 shows us the purpose behind our pain. God doesn't comfort us just to make us feel better - He comforts us so we can become comforters. Some of the most powerful ministry happens when someone who's walked through the valley of depression sits with another sufferer and says, "I know - and here's how God met me there." Our wounds become credentials for ministry. I'll never forget the cancer survivor who visited me after my diagnosis. She didn't offer platitudes - just sat with me and cried, because she knew. That's the kind of comfort only pain can teach us to give.

These four truths form an unshakable foundation when suffering hits. They don't remove the pain, but they do remove the panic. They assure us that our suffering isn't meaningless, even when it feels unbearable. And they remind us that our pain is never wasted in God's economy - it's always being transformed into something far greater than we can imagine.

E. Fake Perseverance: Spiritual Counterfeits to Avoid

In our comfort-craving culture, we've invented cheap substitutes for real perseverance:

1. **Stoic Endurance** - The stiff-upper-lip approach that denies emotions. But Scripture models raw lament (Psalm 22) and Jesus wept openly (John 11:35).
2. **Prosperity Gospel** - The lie that faith guarantees health and wealth. Yet Paul's ministry was marked by beatings and imprisonments (2 Corinthians 11:23-27).
3. **Therapeutic Christianity** - Reducing faith to self-care and happiness. But we're called to share Christ's sufferings (Philippians 3:10).
4. **Political Saviors** - Putting hope in governments rather than Christ's kingdom. Peter reminds we're "strangers and exiles" (1 Peter 2:11).

5. **Digital Distraction** - Numbing ourselves with endless scrolling instead of developing endurance. Scripture calls us to "wait for the Lord" (Psalm 27:14), not escape discomfort.

The Real Deal?

Authentic perseverance is rooted in God's sovereignty, fueled by grace, and fixed on eternity. It's not about gritting our teeth but clinging to Christ - the founder and perfecter of our faith (Hebrews 12:2).

Now that's endurance that lasts.

III. Real-World Perseverance for Today and Tomorrow and the Day After That....

Let's cut through the fluff and talk about what perseverance *actually* looks like when life kicks you in the teeth. This isn't about motivational quotes or Instagram-worthy spirituality—it's about survival tactics for the soul when the storm won't let up.

1. Spiritual Disciplines That Work When You're Barely Holding On

If you want to endure, you need to train like an athlete preparing for the fight of their life. Start by immersing yourself in the gritty survival stories of Scripture—not just reading about Joseph in prison, but *feeling* the damp stone walls, the isolation, the betrayal, and how he kept faith anyway. Memorize passages like Romans 5:3-5 until they're etched into your bones, because when crisis hits, you won't have the mental bandwidth to flip through your Bible looking for comfort. Keep a "God's Faithfulness" journal, but make it real—not some polished devotional, but a raw, unfiltered record of every time God showed up when you were sure He wouldn't.

Prayer can't be a last-resort panic button—it has to be your first reflex. When you're too wrecked to form coherent thoughts, borrow David's prayers from Psalm 13 or Psalm 22. Create emergency spiritual flares—short, punchy anchors like "The Lord is my helper" (Hebrews 13:6)—that you can cling to when the waves are crashing over your head. And when even that feels impossible, practice "breath prayers"—single exhales of "Jesus... mercy..." that keep you tethered to Him when words fail.

But you can't do this alone. You need a **"Perseverance Posse"**—three or four people who know your struggles, won't let you quit, and will call you out when you start spiraling. This isn't about polite small talk; it's about the early church model of radical burden-bearing (Galatians 6:2), which means actual meals when you're sick, job leads when you're unemployed, and middle-of-the-night phone calls when the darkness feels suffocating. Establish a "100% honesty, zero judgment" rule, because fake smiles and vague prayer requests won't cut it when the stakes are this high.

2. Enduring When the Trial Has No Expiration Date

Chronic illness isn't just a physical battle—it's a spiritual gauntlet. If your body is failing you, take a page from Paul's playbook in 2 Corinthians 12:7-10 and reframe your weakness as the very thing that forces you to rely on Christ's strength. Build a "Low-Energy Toolkit"—audio Bible for migraine days, coloring prayer journals for shaky hands, and worship playlists for when you can't muster the energy to pray. And don't let your limitations fool you into thinking you're useless—your hospital bed might just become a prayer command center for others fighting similar battles.

Financial freefall will test your faith like nothing else. When the bank account's empty and the bills keep coming, practice "radical gratitude"—naming three specific provisions each day, even if it's just that you woke up breathing. Conduct a "Needs vs. Wants" autopsy—

that daily Starbucks isn't evil, but learning to live without it isn't deprivation, it's spiritual archaeology, stripping away the nonessentials to uncover what really matters.

And then there's relational warfare—toxic family, backstabbing friends, or abusive bosses. Jesus told us to be "wise as serpents and innocent as doves" (Matthew 10:16), which means learning to love without being a doormat. Develop a "Persecutor Prayer Protocol"—bless them sincerely, then set boundaries firmly. Pursue reconciliation like a detective—seeking truth first, peace second (Romans 12:18)—because some bridges can't be rebuilt overnight, and that's okay.

3. Raising the Next Generation to Outlast the Storm

Kids won't learn perseverance from sanitized Sunday school stories. They need raw, unfiltered hero tales—like Corrie ten Boom watching her sister die in Ravensbrück, yet still choosing forgiveness. Create "Faithfulness Badges" to celebrate everyday courage—sticking with hard homework counts as much as Bible memorization. And normalize struggle by letting them see *your* battles—how you pray through layoffs, marital tension, or your own doubts.

Teens need pressure-tested faith, not platitudes. Host "Apocalypse Dinner Table Debates"—grill them on why God allows suffering while you pass the mashed potatoes. Create "Pressure Cooker Scenarios"—role-play defending their faith to a hostile professor or resisting peer pressure in a party situation. And analyze cultural lies together—compare Instagram's highlight reels to Paul's shipwreck resume in 2 Corinthians 11.

Young adults are walking into a world that's openly hostile to biblical values. Prep them for workplace persecution—what will they do when asked to compromise ethics for a promotion? Teach them "Financial Krav Maga"—how to dodge debt traps and live countercultually in a buy-now-pay-later culture. And model

"Marathon Marriage"—let them see you fight fair, reconcile after decades, and choose love when feelings fade.

4. Emergency Protocols for When the Wheels Come Off

For terminal diagnoses, create a "Legacy of Hope" kit—letters, videos, and Scripture recordings for loved ones. Develop a "Pain Scale Prayer System"—from whispered thanks on tolerable days to screaming Psalms when the agony is unbearable.

For spiritual burnout, establish "Red Line Triggers"—when you hit these warning signs (like skipping prayer for two weeks or isolating yourself), your posse intervenes. Schedule a "Reboot Retreat"—24 hours with no demands, just you and God in the woods, recalibrating your soul.

And if cultural collapse comes, be ready. Build a "Digital Ark"—preserve core Scriptures and teachings offline in case the internet goes dark. Learn "House Church Basics"—how to baptize, break bread, and lead when institutions crumble.

The Bottom Line: Perseverance isn't inspirational—it's *instinctual*. It's the gut-level refusal to let go of God, even when every fiber of your being wants to quit. It's storing truth like a prepper stores food, building community like a platoon that depends on each other, and developing contingency plans for when all hell breaks loose.

This isn't just survival training—it's *warrior* training. The storm is coming. Are you ready?

IV. Wrapping It Up: Why Hanging On Now Pays Off Forever

Modern life isn't for the faint of heart. While the world scrambles for quick fixes and instant highs, our stubborn refusal to quit will stand out like fireworks in a blackout (Philippians 2:15). Here's the kicker: Every ounce of endurance you're scraping together today is actually building an eternal reward that'll make your current struggles look like lightweights (2 Corinthians 4:17).

Your Game Plan for the Long Haul

First, run a **"Perseverance Check-Up"**—where are you most likely to tap out? Is it when the money's tight? When relationships blow up? When the culture keeps moving the goalposts? Name your weak spots now so they don't blindside you later.

Next, lock arms with a few **battle buddies**—not just casual small group friends, but ride-or-die believers who'll call you out when you start making excuses and pull you back up when you faceplant. Set regular check-ins where "How's your walk with God?" gets traded for "No really—how are you *actually* holding up?"

And here's a power move: **Start a "God's Track Record" file**. Jot down every time He's come through—the job He provided last minute, the diagnosis that turned around, the relationship He restored. Future you will need this evidence when new storms hit.

The Finish Line Is Worth It

This race is a marathon, not a sprint—but Jesus already blazed the trail (Hebrews 12:2). He endured the cross knowing what was on the other side, and here's the mind-blowing part: *Your perseverance is banking eternal glory that'll make today's worst moments fade in comparison* (Romans 8:18).

So when the world asks why you bother sticking with hard truths, difficult relationships, or unpopular convictions, remember—you're not just surviving, you're storing up a reward that'll outlast every trend, crisis, and cultural earthquake.

Nine Words that Change Everything

Keep your knees dirty from praying, your hands calloused from serving, and your heart tethered to the One who's waiting at the finish line. The best is yet to come.

Chapter 9:

Presence – Experiencing the Nearness of God in Everyday Life

I. What Does the Bible Really Mean by God's Presence?

Let's talk about something mind-blowing—the Bible's picture of God's presence isn't some abstract idea, but a reality that changes everything. From the very beginning, we see God didn't just create the world and step back—He walked in the garden with Adam and Eve (Genesis 3:8), setting the pattern for the kind of intimate relationship He's always wanted with us.

But then sin wrecked that closeness. The beautiful thing is, the rest of Scripture shows God relentlessly working to restore it. He showed up personally to Abraham (Genesis 12:7), appeared to Moses in a burning bush, and filled the tabernacle with His glory (Exodus 40:34-38). When Solomon dedicated the temple, fire fell from heaven (2 Chronicles 7:1-3)—proof God still wanted to dwell with His people.

Then came the game-changer: Jesus. John 1:14 says He "became flesh and moved into the neighborhood." God wasn't just visiting—He was here to stay. And after Jesus ascended, He sent the Holy Spirit at Pentecost (Acts 2:1-4), fulfilling His promise to never leave us (John 14:16-17). Now here's the crazy part: Paul says *we* are God's temple—both together as the Church (1 Corinthians 3:16) and individually as believers (1 Corinthians 6:19).

The Bible shows God's presence in three life-changing ways:

1. **Omnipresence**—He's everywhere, holding everything together (Psalm 139:7-12).

2. **Manifest Glory**—Those awe-inspiring moments when He shows up unmistakably, like at Mount Sinai (Exodus 24:15-18).

3. **Indwelling Relationship**—The Holy Spirit living in us, changing us from the inside out (Galatians 2:20).

And here's the kicker—God's presence *always* transforms people. Moses' face shone after meeting with Him (Exodus 34:29). Isaiah was purified when he saw the Lord's glory (Isaiah 6:5-7). The disciples went from hiding in fear to preaching boldly (Acts 4:13).

This isn't just theology—it's an invitation. The same God who filled the temple wants to fill *you*. Not just to visit, but to stay. And when He does, you won't stay the same.

Now that's good news.

II. Experiencing God's Presence: A Deep Dive into How the Trinity Makes Himself Known

Let's have a real conversation about what it means to experience God's presence—not as some abstract theological concept, but as the living, breathing reality that changes everything about how we live. This isn't about checking religious boxes; it's about understanding how the Father, Son, and Holy Spirit each play distinct but perfectly synchronized roles in making God's presence tangible in our lives.

A. The Trinity's Symphony of Presence

Imagine a masterfully orchestrated symphony where each instrument plays its part to create something beautiful. That's how the Trinity works in making God's presence known to us.

1. **The Father's Sustaining Presence** The Bible tells us that God the Father "upholds the universe by the word of His power" (Hebrews 1:3). This means every breath you take, every sunrise you see, and every heartbeat in your chest is sustained by Him. He's not distant or disinterested; He's actively holding everything together, including you.

2. **The Son's Incarnate Presence** Then there's Jesus—God in flesh, who stepped into our broken world to rescue us. Matthew 1:23 calls Him "Immanuel," which means "God with us." He didn't just send a message or a rulebook; He came Himself, walked our roads, felt our pain, and ultimately gave His life to bring us back to God.

3. **The Spirit's Indwelling Presence** After Jesus ascended, He sent the Holy Spirit to live inside believers (Romans 8:9-11). This isn't a metaphor—the Spirit actually takes up residence in you, guiding, comforting, and empowering you from the inside out.

Old Testament Glimpses

Even before Jesus walked the earth, we see hints of this Trinitarian presence. Theophanies (appearances of God) in the Old Testament—like the visitors who met Abraham in Genesis 18 or the Angel of the Lord in Exodus 23—were likely pre-incarnate appearances of Jesus. Meanwhile, the Spirit empowered specific people for specific tasks, like the craftsmen who built the tabernacle (Exodus 31:3) or Gideon when he led Israel (Judges 6:34).

New Testament Fulfillment

Jesus promised His disciples, "I will not leave you as orphans; I will come to you" (John 14:18). He kept that promise at Pentecost (Acts 2), when the Holy Spirit came in power, turning timid followers into bold witnesses. Paul's prayer in Ephesians 3:14-19 captures this beautifully: He asks that we'd be "strengthened with power through [the] Spirit," that "Christ may dwell in [our] hearts," and that we'd be "filled with all the fullness of God."

This changes everything. Christianity isn't about following rules; it's about being in relationship with the living God. It's not about what we do for God but what He's done—and is doing—in us.

B. The Life-Changing Power of God's Presence

Every time someone in Scripture truly encountered God, they walked away fundamentally different. These weren't just spiritual highs; they were transformative experiences that reshaped lives.

1. **Moses at the Burning Bush (Exodus 3)** Moses wasn't looking for God that day—he was just tending sheep. But when God showed up in that burning bush, everything changed. Moses got more than a mission; he got a revelation of God's nature ("I AM WHO I AM") that redefined his entire life.

2. **Isaiah's Temple Vision (Isaiah 6)** Isaiah saw the Lord "high and lifted up," surrounded by angels crying, "Holy, holy, holy!" His immediate reaction? "Woe is me! I am ruined!" (v. 5). God's holiness exposed Isaiah's sinfulness, but it didn't leave him there. A burning coal touched his lips, purging his guilt and commissioning him to speak for God.

3. **Peter's Awakening (Luke 5:8)** After a miraculous catch of fish, Peter fell at Jesus' feet and said, "Go away from me, Lord;

I am a sinful man!" That's what happens when you realize you're in the presence of holiness—you see yourself clearly. But Jesus didn't reject Peter; He called him to something greater.

4. **Pentecost Power (Acts 2)** The disciples went from hiding in fear to preaching with unshakable boldness—not because they mustered up courage but because the Holy Spirit filled them. This wasn't just emotional hype; it was a complete overhaul of their minds, wills, and emotions.

How Transformation Happens

God's presence doesn't just make us feel good; it changes us from the inside out. Here's how:

- **Conviction of Sin (John 16:8):** The Holy Spirit shines a light on what's broken in us, not to shame us but to heal us.
- **Illumination of Truth (John 16:13):** He helps us understand Scripture in ways we couldn't on our own.
- **Grace for Weakness (2 Corinthians 12:9):** When we're at our limit, His power shows up strongest.
- **Purpose in Pain (Philippians 3:10):** Even our suffering gets redeemed, becoming part of our spiritual growth.

The result? We start to look more like Jesus every day (2 Corinthians 3:18), until the day we see Him face to face and the transformation completes (1 John 3:2).

C. Spotting Counterfeits: What Real Presence Isn't

In a world hungry for spiritual experiences, plenty of fakes masquerade as the real thing. Here's how to tell the difference:

1. **Emotionalism** chases feelings—goosebumps, tears, euphoria—without lasting change. Real encounters with

God engage your mind, will, *and* emotions, leading to deeper obedience.

2. **Mysticism** elevates personal impressions above Scripture. While God can speak through dreams or nudges, anything truly from Him will never contradict His Word (Isaiah 8:20).

3. **Ritualism** mistakes going through motions for relationship. Jesus called this out: "These people honor me with their lips, but their hearts are far from me" (Matthew 15:8).

4. **Narcissism** treats God as a means to self-improvement. The gospel isn't about boosting your self-esteem; it's about dying to self and finding life in Christ (Luke 9:23).

5. **Syncretism** blends Christianity with other spiritual practices—like "Christian yoga" or meditation techniques borrowed from Eastern religions. God calls His people to worship Him *only*, without mixing in other beliefs (Deuteronomy 12:30-31).

The Antidote?

Test everything (1 John 4:1). Real encounters with God's presence will always:

- **Align with Scripture**
- **Produce Christlike humility**
- **Point to Jesus, not our own experiences**

The Bottom Line: God's presence isn't a fleeting emotion or a religious routine—it's the Trinity moving into your life, transforming you from the inside out. The Father holds you, the Son redeems you, and the Spirit empowers you. And while counterfeits abound, the real thing leaves you unmistakably, irrevocably changed.

This is what you were made for—to know God and be known by Him. Don't settle for anything less.

III. Making God's Presence Real in Your Everyday Life

Let's get practical—how do we actually live aware of God's presence when life feels anything but spiritual? Here's how to cultivate that awareness and break through the barriers that keep us from experiencing Him.

1. Training Yourself to Notice God

We're surrounded by distractions, but that doesn't mean God's gone silent. The key is building habits that keep us tuned in.

Start with something as simple as the *Jesus Prayer*—"Lord Jesus Christ, Son of God, have mercy on me, a sinner." It's a biblical way to "pray without ceasing" (1 Thessalonians 5:17), turning even mundane moments into conversations with God. Or try *breath prayers*—pairing short Scripture phrases like "Abba, I belong to You" with your breathing. Suddenly, something as automatic as inhaling and exhaling becomes a reminder of His nearness.

Then there's your environment. Place Scripture where you'll see it—on your mirror, fridge, or phone lock screen. Some people even set an empty chair at the table as a physical reminder: *Christ is here with us.*

Brother Lawrence, a 17th-century monk, famously turned dishwashing into worship by doing it "for love of Him." That's the idea—ordinary tasks become sacred when done with awareness of God's presence. Try dedicating routine activities (commuting, workouts, chores) as "presence practice" times.

And yes, even tech can help if used wisely. Prayer reminder apps, Scripture alerts, or worship playlists can redirect your focus upward. But balance it with *digital fasts*—regular breaks from screens to reset your soul in silence.

2. Breaking Down What's Blocking You

We all hit walls that make God feel distant. Here's how to push through: **Digital Overload** Our brains are trained to jump from notification to notification. Fight back with *tech-free zones*—no phones at meals, in bed, or during prayer. Psalm 101:3's "I will set no worthless thing before my eyes" wasn't written for the Instagram age, but it sure applies. **Unconfessed Sin** Isaiah 59:2 is blunt: sin creates distance. The Puritans had a habit of daily "sin autopsy"—reflecting on where they'd failed and bringing it to God immediately. Don't let small compromises pile up; keep *short accounts* with Him. **Doubt** When God feels absent, preach truth to yourself. Memorize Psalm 139:7-12— *"Where can I flee from Your presence?"*—or read stories of how God showed up for others in Scripture and history. **Broken Relationships** Jesus said unresolved conflict with others blocks our connection with God (Matthew 5:23-24). Make peace where possible—not always easy, but always worth it. **Exhaustion** Sometimes, spiritual dryness is just physical burnout. You're not a ghost—you have a body, and neglecting sleep, food, or exercise can numb your spiritual senses just like unconfessed sin (1 Corinthians 6:19-20).

"Sacred Pause" – A 3-Minute Presence Exercise

In the rush of life, it's easy to miss the quiet, constant reality of God's presence. We forget that He is with us, not just in grand moments, but in the ordinary, the messy, and the mundane. This simple 3-minute exercise helps you reset, to step out of the noise and into the awareness that Emmanuel, "God with us," is nearer than your next breath.

Think of this as a spiritual exhale, a chance to release distraction and recenter your heart on the One who promises, "I am with you always" (Matthew 28:20). Whether you use it as a daily rhythm or an emergency anchor in chaotic moments, the "Sacred Pause" invites you to practice His presence right where you are.

Ready? Let's pause.

Step 1: Stillness (1 minute)

Close your eyes. Place both feet flat on the ground and rest your hands open on your lap. Breathe slowly three times—inhale through your nose (4 seconds), hold (4 seconds), exhale through your mouth (6 seconds). Whisper: "God, I'm here with You."

Step 2: Awareness (1 minute)

Ask yourself:

- Where have I sensed God's presence today? (A sunrise? A kind word?)
- Where have I missed Him? (In my hurry? In my frustration?)
- Don't judge—just notice.

Step 3: Invitation (1 minute)

Place one hand over your heart. Pray:

"Jesus, make Your nearness undeniable to me right now. Help me recognize You in…"

(Name one ordinary moment ahead—your next meeting, chore, or decision.)

Close: Open your eyes and carry this prayer with you: "You are here—therefore I am present too." Use a sticky note or a worry stone, or a clinging cross in your pocket to remind yourself to **pause for presence.**

3. Passing It On to the Next Generation

Kids and teens won't learn to seek God's presence by accident. Here's how to teach them at every stage: **For Little Kids (3-10)** Make it tangible. Light a candle while talking about God as light (1 John 1:5). Let them feel different textures while you explain He's always near. Sing simple Scripture songs or keep a "God sightings" journal—recording answered prayers and everyday blessings. **For Preteens (10-13)** Get interactive. Take prayer walks and point out where they might see God at work—in nature, in kindness between friends. Let them draw or paint verses about God's presence. Role-play biblical encounters with God (Moses at the burning bush, Elijah hearing the whisper). **For Teens (14-18)** Give them real spiritual tools. Teach them *lectio divina* (a slow, reflective way to read Scripture). Start prayer journals with prompts like *"Where did I sense God today?"* Get them serving—Jesus said when we care for others, it's Him we're loving (Matthew 25:40).

For Young Adults (18-30), They need mentors who show what integrated faith looks like. Spiritual direction—helping them discern God's voice. Accountability for spiritual habits. Conversations about seeing God in their work or studies. **The Common Thread?** Kids spot fake faith a mile away. The most powerful teaching isn't a lesson—it's *you*, living aware of God's presence in ordinary moments. Family traditions (meal prayers, bedtime blessings, holiday rituals) create spaces where His nearness feels as real as the air they breathe. **Bottom Line:** God's presence isn't just for monks or missionaries—it's for *you*, in your chaos, your commute, your crisis. Train yourself to notice Him, tear down what blocks you, and show the next generation what walking with God really looks like.

This is the difference between knowing about *God and* actually *knowing* Him.

IV. Wrapping It Up: The Best Is Yet to Come

Let's end this where everything is headed—the mind-blowing reality that one day, we'll see God face to face (Revelation 22:4). That's not just some far-off dream; it changes *everything* about how we live right now. All those moments we've spent seeking God—the prayers, the Scripture musings, the quiet pauses in our chaotic days—they're not just religious chores. They're rehearsals for eternity.

Think about David's words: *"In your presence there is fullness of joy"* (Psalm 16:11). That's not poetic exaggeration. It's the truth we're wired for. Every spiritual habit we've talked about? They're like tuning our hearts to a song we'll sing forever.

Here's the wildest part: The same God who crafted the cosmos *chooses* to make His home with us (John 14:23). Let that sink in. It reshapes how we work, love, suffer, and hope. The presence that walks with us through life's darkest valleys now is the very presence that will welcome us into unshakable glory later.

For now, we're like travelers passing through (1 Peter 2:11), but we're carrying something priceless inside us—God's own presence (2 Corinthians 4:7). That's the secret Paul couldn't stop talking about: *"Christ in you, the hope of glory"* (Colossians 1:27).

Your Game Plan for Life on Earth:

1. **Bible Truths to Lock Down** Burn Psalm 139:7-12 and Matthew 28:20b into your memory. These aren't just verses; they're lifelines for when God feels distant.

2. **Everyday Reminders** Set alarms labeled *"God's here"*, slap sticky notes on your dashboard, or sync breath prayers to your commute. Outsmart your distracted brain.

3. **Share the Stories** Once a week, tell someone—your family, your small group, a friend—about one moment you *knew*

God showed up. These "God-sightings" build faith like nothing else.

4. **Schedule Soul Space** Block two hours monthly for uninterrupted time with God. No agenda, no multitasking—just you, His presence, and maybe a journal.

5. **Leave a Trail** Start a "Faithfulness Journal"—not for you, but for your kids, your friends, the people who'll need proof later that God *shows up*.

The Bottom Line: Christianity isn't about rules or rituals. It's about *presence*—God with us, and us waking up to that reality. Every ordinary moment is a chance to encounter Him. Every hard circumstance is training ground to know Him deeper.

As we step into the future, let's live like people who've discovered David's secret: *"You make known to me the path of life; in your presence there is fullness of joy; at your right hand are pleasures forevermore"* (Psalm 16:11).

The journey isn't always easy, but the destination? *Absolutely worth it.*

Chapter 10:

Living the Nine Words

Living the Nine Words Tomorrow and Beyond

1. Preach Propitiation Boldly

In an age that downplays sin and wrath, we must proclaim **propitiation** unapologetically. The cross is not just a symbol of love but the place where justice was served. Let us:

- **Explain why Christ's death was necessary (Romans 6:23).**
- **Reject watered-down gospels that ignore God's holiness.**
- **Lead sinners to see their need for a Savior.**

2. Live a Life of Praise

Praise should permeate our daily lives, not just Sunday services. Practical ways to cultivate praise:

- **Begin each day thanking God for salvation.**
- **Sing hymns or worship songs in times of stress.**
- **Share testimonies of God's faithfulness with others.**

3. Trust in His Provision

Worry is rampant in uncertain times, but God's **provision** is certain. How to rest in it:

- **Practice generosity, knowing God will supply (2 Corinthians 9:8).**
- **Distinguish between wants and needs—He promises the latter.**
- **Remember past instances of His faithfulness.**

4. Rest in His Protection

Fear dominates many hearts, but believers have divine **protection**. To live fearlessly:

- **Memorize Psalm 91 and claim its promises.**
- **Pray for discernment in spiritual warfare (Ephesians 6:12).**
- **Encourage persecuted saints with the hope of eternal security.**

5. Abide in His Peace

Anxiety is a thief, but Christ's **peace** is our guard. Keys to maintaining peace:

- **Bring every concern to God in prayer (Philippians 4:6).**
- **Meditate on Scripture when fearful (Isaiah 26:3).**
- **Avoid obsessive consumption of fear-driven media.**

6. Stand on His Promises

God's **promises** are our anchor in shifting times. How to hold fast:

- **Study covenant promises in Scripture (e.g., Jeremiah 29:11).**
- **Journal moments when God proved faithful.**
- **Preach promises to yourself when discouraged.**

7. Walk in His Power

Self-reliance fails, but God's **power** sustains. To rely on Him:

- **Pray for the Spirit's filling daily (Ephesians 5:18).**
- **Step out in faith where human strength is insufficient.**
- **Serve others in love, trusting God for the results.**

8. Persevere in Trials

Hardship is inevitable, but **perseverance** proves genuine faith. How to endure:

- **Fix your eyes on Christ (Hebrews 12:2).**
- **Lean on the church for support (Galatians 6:2).**
- **Remember: trials are temporary; glory is eternal (Romans 8:18).**

9. Cultivate His Presence

Without **presence**, faith becomes ritual. To abide in Him:

- **Practice "prayer without ceasing" (1 Thessalonians 5:17).**
- **Study Scripture devotionally, not just intellectually.**
- **Prioritize corporate worship (Hebrews 10:25).**

Final Encouragement

These nine words are not just theology—they are the heartbeat of the Christian life. As tomorrow unfolds, may we live them out with ever-deepening faith, knowing that "He who began a good work in [us] will carry it on to completion" (Philippians 1:6).

To God be the glory!

Conclusion

When Nine Words (Plus One) Change Everything

We began this journey with nine words that form the unshakable foundation of our faith. Propitiation—because the cross makes everything else possible. Praise—our inevitable response to such staggering grace. Provision, protection, peace—God's daily gifts to His children. Promise, power, perseverance—the fuel for our journey. And presence—the beautiful reality that Emmanuel is with us always.

But there's a bonus word that ties them all together: Providence.

Romans 8:28 declares, "And we know that in all things God works for the good of those who love Him, who have been called according to His purpose." This isn't just a comforting thought; it's the heartbeat of God's sovereign care. Providence means He doesn't just react to our circumstances; He orchestrates them for His glory and our ultimate good.

Let's trace this thread through each of our nine words in greater depth:

1. Propitiation (John 1:29; Romans 3:25)

Providence's Role: The cross was not Plan B. Before creation, God ordained Christ as "the Lamb slain from the foundation of the world" (Revelation 13:8). Providence ensured that every detail—the timing (Galatians 4:4), the prophecies (Isaiah 53), even the wrath Jesus would bear—was meticulously arranged.

Why It Matters: Your salvation isn't a happy accident. The same Providence that planned redemption guarantees its effects in your life: "He who did not spare His own Son... how will He not also... graciously give us all things?" (Romans 8:32).

2. Praise (Psalm 145:3)

Providence's Role: Worship isn't just a response to blessings; it's the recognition that every blessing flows from God's sovereign hand. Providence turns even suffering into a platform for praise (Acts 16:25, Paul and Silas in prison).

Why It Matters: When you grasp that God intentionally shepherds your life (Psalm 23:1), praise becomes involuntary—like David declaring, "Surely goodness and mercy shall follow me all the days of my life" (Psalm 23:6).

3. Provision (Philippians 4:19)

Providence's Role: God doesn't just react to your needs; He anticipates them. He fed Elijah via ravens (1 Kings 17:4), multiplied loaves (Matthew 14:20), and promises to supply "all your need" (not all your wants) according to His purposes.

Why It Matters: Providence means your lack is not oversight—it's opportunity. "Your Father knows what you need before you ask Him" (Matthew 6:8).

4. Protection (Psalm 91:1-2)

Providence's Role: God doesn't promise a danger-free life but purpose-filled deliverance. He shut lions' mouths for Daniel (Daniel 6:22) and walked with Shadrach in the fire (Daniel 3:25)—not always from harm, but through it.

Why It Matters: Even when evil seems to win, Providence assures: "No weapon formed against you shall prosper" (Isaiah 54:17). Your trials are filtered by His hands.

5. Peace (John 14:27)

Providence's Role: True peace isn't the absence of storms but the presence of the One who rules them (Mark 4:39). Providence means "all things", even chaos, serve His plan (Romans 8:28).

Why It Matters: When anxiety screams, Providence whispers: "I have calmed and quieted my soul" (Psalm 131:2). Your circumstances may not change, but your heart can.

6. Promise (2 Corinthians 1:20)

Providence's Role: Every covenant God makes is secured by His sovereignty. Abraham's descendants outnumbered stars (Genesis 15:5), and Christ's return is just as certain (Revelation 22:20).

Why It Matters: Providence ensures "not one word has failed of all His good promise" (1 Kings 8:56). His Word is your anchor.

7. Power (Acts 1:8)

Providence's Role: The Spirit's power isn't for your agenda but His kingdom. Samson's strength (Judges 16:28) and Paul's endurance (2 Corinthians 12:9) were both fueled by divine strategy.

Why It Matters: You're not left to self-help. "His divine power has given us everything we need for life and godliness" (2 Peter 1:3).

8. Perseverance (Hebrews 12:1-2)

Providence's Role: Your faith isn't sustained by willpower but by "Him who is able to keep you from stumbling" (Jude 1:24). Even Peter's denial was woven into redemption (Luke 22:31-32).

Why It Matters: Providence guarantees: "He who began a good work in you will carry it to completion" (Philippians 1:6).

9. Presence (Matthew 28:20)

Providence's Role: God doesn't just watch your journey; He inhabits it. The pillar of fire (Exodus 13:21) and the Emmaus road (Luke 24:15) reveal His intentional nearness.

Why It Matters: Providence means you're never alone: "I am with you always" (Matthew 28:20)—not as a spectator, but as the Author.

Why This Changes Everything

- **Your past? Redeemed by Providence.**
- **Your trials? Filtered by Providence.**
- **Your future? Held by Providence.**

This isn't blind optimism; it's blood-bought certainty. The God who gave His Son for you (Romans 8:32) is the same God scripting your story with perfect wisdom.

Here's the breathtaking reality: The same God who orchestrated your salvation through Christ's propitiation is now orchestrating every detail of your life with perfect providence. **Your mistakes? Redeemable. Your pain? Purposeful. Your waiting? Preparatory.**

So here's your takeaway: **These nine words + God's providence = unshakable confidence for whatever comes next. Now go live like you believe it!**

Amen and Amen!

Afterword

"Prayer—The Breath of All Nine Words and the Bridge to Providence"

When the chapters close and bookmarks are laid aside, the silence finally comes, not as a question, but as an invitation. It is the moment when the ninth word gives way to a tenth that always existed forever. Now we finally look at a heavily mentioned word in endless Christian self-help books that never needed to be printed on paper: Prayer. The invisible conductor leading the symphony of all other words: Propitiation, Praise, Provision, Protection, Peace, Promise, Power, Perseverance, Presence—into living, breathing reality.

Prayer is not the accompaniment; it is the oxygen. It is the unseen current flowing beneath every storyline, threading every verse into the tapestry of God's sovereign plan.

Prayer as the Catalyst—Acting as the Conduit:

Think of prayer as the unseen pipe linking every wire of the nine-word circuit to Divine electricity. When we pray with the heart of propitiation, we are not just repeating doctrines—we are connecting the flame to the fuse. Grace becomes more than theology—it becomes living blood surging through veins.

Prayer as the Continuous Conversation:

Prayer is the never-ending dialogue between heaven and earth. It is the gentle whisper that says, "This is not just verse or chapter—it is the very essence of your life enacted." In the conversation with the Father, accusations melt into absolution, fears fade into faith, and doubts dissolve into declaration. Provision, protection, peace—they flow into the bloodstream of our daily life, activated by the simple act of communion with the Creator.

Prayer as Uncensored Dialogue:

When we pray without ceasing, we step into the throne room, speaking the language of grace into the corners of our lives and the corners of our hearts. Here, every tear becomes a testimony, every sigh a sermon. We no longer just read the Scriptures; we live them.

Prayer As a Dialogue with Purpose:

Prayer is the tongue that speaks the language of grace into the rhythm of our days and the heartbeat of our existence.

Prayer in the Ever-Present:

When we pray, we are not perplexed; we are anchored. When we pray without ceasing, we step into the throne room where every tear becomes a testimony and every sigh a sermon. We are no longer just reading the Word; we are living it. In the very breath of prayer lies the whispered power that binds every leaf to the vine, every stem to the branch, keeping the believer rooted, alive, and fruitful. It is the quiet conductor ensuring that every beat of life pulses with the steady rhythm of divine grace.

And so, the chapter closes, not with a period, but with a promise: a promise that every step you take into the unknown will be cradled in continual, unceasing prayer—until at last, every whispered prayer becomes an eternal echo of thanksgiving, every breath becomes a living testimony to the God who is now, ever, and always Emmanuel, within you and beside you, here and now.

Forever. Amen.

www.ingramcontent.com/pod-product-compliance
Lightning Source LLC
Chambersburg PA
CBHW071235090426
42736CB00014B/3094